CAFE

PASQUAL'S

COOKBOOK

CAFE
PASQUAL'S
COOKBOOK

Spirited Recipes from Santa Fe

by Katharine Kagel

Photographs by Barbara Simpson

Cafe Pasqual's

CHRONICLE BOOKS

SAN FRANCISCO

Library of Congress Cataloging-in-Publication Data:
Kagel, Katharine.
    Cafe Pasqual's cookbook : spirited recipes from Sante Fe / by
  Katharine Kagel ; photographs by Barbara Simpson.
        p. cm.
  ISBN 0-8118-0293-0
  1. Cafe Pasqual. 2. Cookery, American—Southwestern style.
  3. Cookery, Mexican. I. Title.
TX715.2.S69K35 1993
641.59789—dc20   92-41350
                        CIP

Printed in Hong Kong

Editing: Sharon Silva
Murals: Leovigildo Martinez
Design: Julie Noyes Long
Hand-lettering: David Coulson
Typesetting: TBH Typecast, Inc.
Photograph of Cafe Pasqual's Mural: Cissie Ludlow

Distributed in Canada by Raincoast Books
9050 Shaughnessy Street, Vancouver, B.C. V6P 6E5

10

Chronicle Books LLC
85 Second Street
San Francisco, CA 94105

www.chroniclebooks.com

*This book
is for my three kitchen muses—
my mother, Sophia, my grandmother Maga, and Della—
with love and gratitude.*

TABLE OF CONTENTS

ACKNOWLEDGMENTS

*L*ife is a collaboration, cooking a stew pot, a cafe, a beehive. The success and joys of Cafe Pasqual's are due to many wonderful people to whom I give grateful thanks.

I thank my mother, Sophia Kagel, partner in Pasqual's, sage counselor, and fabulous cook, for teaching me always to use the best and freshest ingredients available, and for showing me how to care for guests and guide them through a meal.

I thank my father, Sam Kagel, for teaching me the meaning of *best*—from a hot dog at The Smokehouse to *quenelles* at L'Etoile—for hours of labor relations advice, for sharing his business acumen, and for shoring me up when the tide got too high.

I thank both my parents for teaching me to care for those who are no one's guests, the hungry and less fortunate.

Loving thanks to Maga, grandmother Jenny Kagel, who made food "ritual." And grateful thanks to Della Clay, who, with my mother, was at the center of our family kitchen, and who provided my vital first cooking lessons.

I thank my brother Pete for his interest, ideas, and advice; and my brother John and his wife, Mary Pat, for letting me test in their beautiful kitchen.

Arrigato to Margo Stipe, who began Cafe Pasqual's with me and endured the precarious hard-scrabble early years with energy, unending humor (albeit *noire*), and faith in the future.

My appreciation to Carol Masahara-Page for her patient testing of recipes, and to Karen Frerichs for her savvy styling, recipe testing, and encouragement. Thanks to Linda Schulak, for years and years of telepathic fun and for zillions of hours of recipe development. I owe thanks to Mark Schilkey for "doing the door" all those years, and for his many kindnesses to me and the "kids." Thanks to Mark Matthiessen for his expert feedback. Many thanks to Carroll Johnson for five unforgettable years across the prep island. A toast to Cyndi Tanner, cherished friend, for her original approach to waitressing, and for providing me with hours of ripping good stories. Thanks to B.C. Caldwell for first dreaming Pasqual's. And special thanks to our fairy godmother, Theo Raven, for actually pointing the way.

To our staff in both the dining room and kitchen, past and present, paeans of praise for their stellar hard work. For having conceived of this book and nurtured the blossoming of Cafe Pasqual's, I thank most affectionately Brad Brown, general manager, dear friend, and coconspirator. I am forever indebted to David Coulson, heroic manager, systems and operations engineer, cosmic friend and forecaster.

Blessings on Rudy Gabaldon, the finest breakfast cook on the planet, for his steady, easy spirit. Many thanks to Ricky Gabaldon for working both prep and line with aplomb, and to Gabriel Ruiz for responding with "no problema" to thousands of requests and for cooking awesome quantities of beautiful food these many years. Praises for Presciliano Ruiz for his knowledgeable, faultless, and elegant preparation and cooking skills. Much appreciation to Mike Ewanciw for his hoppin' good spirits. Thanks to Ned Harris for "nailing down" the office, and door, on weekends. Ovations for chef Laura Taylor for her zany wonderful ways, loud laughter, and exhilarating food-art, and laurels for chef Jason Aufrichtig for his creative, stylish plates and his know-how with fish! Hats off to Sally Witham, *chef fantastique,* for her generous contributions to our menu and patrons. Sincere thanks to Anton Balcomb and his crew for cleaning into the wee hours every night, but two, all year. Thank you to Aztec Plumbing—Vance, Jim, and Bear—for being there, and being there, and being there.

My appreciation to Ann Rogers for keeping all the numbers straight, and to Bill Takala for checking the buttons and tying the bows.

Manager, David Coulson, Cafe Pasqual's.

My gratitude to Robert Stricker for his patient good humor. Thanks to Toula Polygalaktos for first faith. Thanks and appreciation to Caroline Herter and Bill LeBlond of Chronicle Books for their trust and guidance, and applause for Leslie Jonath's careful shepherding of this book to final form. *Muchisimas gracias* to Sharon Silva for her thoughtful, comprehensive editing and fine-tuning.

Thanks to Barbara Simpson for documenting Cafe Pasqual's world so artistically with her superb photographs. Kudos to MaLin Wilson and Greg Powell for their marvelous willingness to be guinea pigs on the shortest notice, and bouquets to MaLin for her critical insights and ability to articulate sensibilities. *Abrazos* to John Olesen for his warm counsel and cheer.

Gracias to Anna Walton for her sterling editing and meticulous thought, and for making the last throes of the book project great fun.

Sincerest thanks to our growers, planters, and gatherers who labor so hard for our nourishment and pleasure.

Heartfelt thanks to all the dear friends and patrons of Cafe Pasqual's. Without your patronage and friendship, this book could not have been possible.

Harvest at Delfin's Orchard, Dixon, New Mexico.

Truman Brigham in his lettuce field, Santa Cruz, in the Española Valley in New Mexico.

INTRODUCTION

*F*amily, friends, patrons, cooks, servers, managers, chefs, and neighbors have all contributed to the menu at Pasqual's and to the recipes in this book. I am fortunate indeed to have had the contributions of so many incredibly talented and creative individuals.

Not all of Cafe Pasqual's recipes are here; that would take volumes. But there is a lively sampling, some of which will hopefully become indispensable additions to your repertoire. We have offered all of these dishes over the last fourteen years to our enthusiastic, hungry patrons, an overflowing crowd that includes both local Santa Feans and visitors to our fascinating area. Some of the recipes here are proven standbys and have been on our menu since the beginning. Others appear on the menu as specials. All of them, however, reflect my philosophy that the freshest ingredients must be used to produce dishes that are emphatic and compelling.

I never turn down help in the kitchen! That's why I chose to name the restaurant after the folk saint of Mexican and New Mexican kitchens and cooks, San Pasqual. His image is often seen in Santa Fe kitchens, either painted decoratively on the bowls of wooden spoons or, more often, on a small slab of wood, a *retablo*, hung on the wall.

San Pasqual adorned the wall of my first kitchen in Santa Fe. That was 1978. Within a year of moving here, I opened Cafe Pasqual's. I had visited the city ten years before and instantly felt at home. But school, a marriage, and "life" intervened before I was able to return for good. I never imagined that when my new life finally began here it would include owning and operating a thriving corner cafe in the heart of old Santa Fe.

The idea of the cafe came to me through many conversations with those around me, and with one person in particular. A few weeks after moving to Santa Fe, I walked into a treasure trove of a shop called Doodlet's and struck up a conversation with the proprietress, Theo Raven. We talked for a while, and then I offered her my card. At the time, I was running a catering business called China Catering. She read my card, looked up, and said firmly, "See that restaurant across the street? Go buy it."

I did, forming a partnership with business colleague Margo Stipe for the first six years, the formative and most difficult ones. Margo was a brick, and her stalwart dedication helped build a solid foundation for the cafe.

Cafe Pasqual's is ensconced in a small pueblo-style building, so old that no one knows for certain the origin of its walls. We do know that there have been various habitations on our corner since the 1600s, when the Spanish came and settled Santa Fe.

The cafe is located one block from the plaza, in the heart of the downtown. The dining room walls are lined with hand-painted Mexican tiles, and one whole wall is a mural, by Oaxacan painter Leovigildo Martinez, depicting the Moon reveling at her fiesta. Pasqual's is a small cafe by any standards, seating only fifty at a time, but each day the kitchen makes enormous quantities of the recipes you will find in these pages to feed our many customers. We bake dozens of loaves of bread, churn gallons of ice cream, create chile sauces by the potful, hand-chop the ingredients for crocks of salsas, and perform countless other preparations.

Santa Fe is the second oldest city in the United States, nestled seven thousand feet high in the southernmost tip of the Rocky Mountains. The city has a unique history, being situated at the confluence of several remarkable features. The Rio Grande, the Old Santa Fe Trail trade route, and the royal road from Mexico City all converge here, thus bringing different cultures together. Native Americans, Hispanos, and Anglos have been mingling here for centuries. The local food reflects this mixture, giving rise to a cuisine that is uniquely New Mexican. It is different from Tex-Mex and from the border food that most Americans understand to be Mexican food.

Detail of wall painting entitled La Luna Se Fue a Una Fiesta *by Leovigildo Martinez.*
Depicts partygoer pouring mescal into the mouth of the moon. Cafe Pasqual's, Santa Fe, New Mexico.

The regional foods from New Mexico include traditional red and green chile sauces, pinto beans, squash, *posole*, tortillas, tamales, and various other corn dishes. The dishes from Old Mexico you will find in these pages include egg dishes from both the high-desert ranches and the jungle, a rich chile *mole* sauce from the Puebla region, a *tamal* and a mango recipe interpretation from Oaxaca, a soup from the northern states, and a classic chicken dish from the Yucatán. Salsas, tamales, *asada*, and burritos all have flavors the cafe kitchen has made contemporary, but which are actually derived from ancient sources.

You will also find recipes from Thailand, a favorite cuisine of our kitchen because so many of the ingredients are shared with the Americas—chiles, cilantro, fish, and garlic. For a fascinating study of a worldwide culinary diaspora, follow the chile from its origins in the Americas.

I am frequently asked how we know what quantity of food to order and prepare. We use our experience, but built into most eating establishments is an excess of unserved food. For example, every day at Pasqual's we make more bread, soup, and special items than we think we'll need in order not to run out. We give the surplus to our local perishable and prepared food rescue program, The Food Brigade. The brigade relies on volunteer food runners who transport unserved food to our city's social services agencies and shelters to help feed our hungry neighbors. Restaurants, hotels, caterers, growers, and supermarkets all donate to The Food Brigade. To date there are over a hundred such organizations in North America (the network's international headquarters, The Foodchain, is located in Atlanta, Georgia), and food recycling is becoming a revolution. Just as we at Cafe Pasqual's care about where our food comes from and the people who grow it, so, too, are we concerned that our unserved, perishable food be used to nourish those in need in our community.

Cooks are alchemists, searching for ways to turn food into memories, nourishment, and joy. That's why I cook. That's why you're reading this book. My philosophy, which has guided Cafe Pasqual's for fourteen years, is a simple one: Gather together the best possible staff and ingredients to synergize unforgettable flavors in the most interesting and inspired way, with an eye to healthful preparation methods.

In these pages you will meet Cafe Pasqual's suppliers, the growers of its native and exotic vegetables and fruits, its purveyors, the chile pickers, and a few of its staff members and patrons. You will also be introduced to the food we serve at the cafe—a table that reflects interest in cuisines from many cultures, but has a backbone of recipes from both Mexico and New Mexico.

We hope this compilation of recipes and visual images will bring you new nourishment and joy. Remember, *Panza llena, corazon contento!*—"Full stomach, contented heart!"

NOTES ON INGREDIENTS

ACHIOTE

This is a paste made from the softened seeds of the *annatto* tree, with the addition of vinegar and garlic. It is used as a seasoning and marinade and imparts a reddish hue and earthy character to Mexican dishes. (The *annatto* seed itself is widely used in processed foods, such as butter, to deepen their yellow color.) *Achiote* is packaged in bright orange or terra-cotta "bricks" that are claylike in texture. It is commonly used in the West Indies and the Yucatán peninsula, and is available in this country at Latino markets. There is no substitute.

ASADERO CHEESE

A mild white cheese often sold in loaf form, *asadero* is used extensively in Mexico as a mild melting cheese but is much less available north of the border. Made from half sour and half fresh cow's milk, *asadero* has a subtle flavor all its own. When visiting Mexico, enjoy it melted and accompanied with tomatillo salsa or in a lusty dish called *fundido*, melted *asadero* and crumbled chorizo served with crisp tortilla pieces.

ASIAN SESAME OIL

This dark brown oil is made from toasted sesame seeds and is not the same product as the cold-pressed sesame oil found bottled or in bulk in health-food or natural-food stores. It lends a strong, unique sesame flavor and should be used sparingly. There is no substitute.

CHILE PEPPERS

A descriptive list of all the chile peppers used in the recipes falls at the end of this ingredients section.

CHOCOLATE **See Mexican chocolate.**

CILANTRO

Also known as fresh coriander and Chinese parsley, this is an essential yet controversial herb. One either loves this lively, bright green flat-leafed herb or abhors it. My advice to those who hate it is to take a bite every now and then, because one day, as if by magic, even the most avowed cilantro hater gets hooked and abhorrence turns to addiction. It happened to me. Coriander seed, from which the herb is grown, is not a substitute for the leaf. Indeed, there is no substitute. Store the fragile herb, root end down, in an inch of water with a plastic bag loosely wrapped about the leaves. Use cilantro as soon as possible after purchasing or harvesting. It is easy to grow in a windowbox in the kitchen.

CINNAMON   See Mexican cinnamon.

CLARIFIED BUTTER

At Pasqual's we clarify all butter used for sautéing, pan searing, or whenever melted butter is called for. Clarifying is a simple process that removes the milk solids from the butter. Removing the solids raises the burning point of the butter and makes for improved sautéing, as foods do not tend to stick to the pan. Since rancid butter is caused by milk solids spoiling, removing them also guarantees better flavor and increases the butter's storage life. To clarify butter, bring at least 1 pound of butter to a boil in a saucepan. Boil about 5 minutes. Skim the foam off the top and discard. The milk solids will settle to the bottom of the pan. Pour the remaining clear yellow liquid through a cheesecloth-lined strainer into a storage container (preferably glass) and cover tightly. Clarified butter will keep for months in the refrigerator or freezer.

FISH SAUCE   See Thai fish sauce.

KAFFIR LIME LEAVES

These dried lime leaves imported from Thailand add a delicious sour-sweet flavor to soups, sauces, and stews. They are widely available from Asian markets and gourmet groceries. There is no substitute.

LEMONGRASS

When sold fresh, this elongated grasslike herb is 9 to 12 inches in length and about 3/4 of an inch in diameter. It resembles a green onion, but is more tannish green and has more fibrous leaves. Use only the white bulb portion; discard the tough upper leaves. Lemongrass becomes soggy once it is frozen, so freeze it only if there is no reliable fresh source. At Pasqual's we precut it into 1/4-inch-thick rounds for freezing if we know our source is temporarily drying up. Lemongrass can be found in Asian markets and in the produce departments of large supermarkets. If neither source is available in your community, ask to have it special ordered. Do not substitute shredded dried lemongrass or dried lemongrass tea leaves.

MEXICAN CHOCOLATE

This dark chocolate is processed with cinnamon, ground almonds, and granulated sugar. Mexican chocolate is traditionally used to make hot chocolate and is often foamed using a wooden implement called a *molinillo*. Mexican chocolate is packaged in 3-ounce tablets and is available in Latino markets, the Mexican-food section of large supermarkets, gourmet grocery stores, and through mail-order sources.

MEXICAN CINNAMON

Mexican cinnamon, or *canela*, is not commonly used in North America. It is much softer than the widely used, nearly rock-hard stick cinnamon. The softer inner bark of Mexican cinnamon is easily ground into a powder and its sweet flavor is pleasantly distinctive. Look for it in Latino markets, the Mexican-food section of large supermarkets, gourmet grocery stores, and through mail-order sources.

MEXICAN OREGANO

Mexican oregano is difficult to find, but can be obtained through mail-order sources. The oregano stocked in most American supermarkets is Greek oregano and is much stronger in flavor than the Mexican variety. The leaf marjoram widely sold in the United States more closely approximates the subtle flavor of Mexican oregano, however, and may be substituted for it. (Try leaf marjoram in other recipes that call for oregano and you may be won over by its gentler taste.)

PIÑON NUT

Piñon trees are small pines that dot the landscape in New Mexico and throughout the desert Southwest. They grow at elevations above 5,000 feet and bear cones that conceal sweet and quite oily pine nuts, or *piñones*. The nuts are so oily, in fact, that in the past in Korea, where they are also native, they were strung on long strings and used for lighting homes. (To see for yourself, put a pine nut on the end of a straight pin and light it. It should burn for about 2 minutes!) Pine nuts, because they are harvested by hand, are quite costly. They are imported from China and are found in bulk in health-food markets. European pine nuts, commonly called pignolias (from the Italian *pinoli* or *pignoli*), are also imported and are more dear than their Asian cousins. The Native Americans and Spanish have used the piñon nut ground as a flour and whole as a winter snack for centuries.

POSOLE

Posole (sometimes spelled *pozole*) are white dried or fresh-frozen large corn kernels, commonly called hominy, that have been processed in a lime solution to remove the hulls. *Posole* is the Spanish name for hominy and is also the name for the stewed dish made from hominy that is served either as an accompaniment or as a main course. Canned hominy may not be substituted for dried or fresh-frozen *posole*; it does not have the same "corn" flavor. For Hispanos and Native Americans of New Mexico, *posole* is a traditional part of holiday feasts. Depending upon the occasion, the dish can be quite simple or it can be complicated, with many ingredients and condiments. *Posole* is available in Latino markets and in the Mexican-food section of larger supermarkets. Dried *posole* may be ordered by mail.

SESAME OIL   See Asian sesame oil.

THAI FISH SAUCE

There are many brands of Thai fish sauce, called *nam pla*, on the market. Their saltiness varies, so try different labels until you find one you like. There is no substitute for this wonderful and essential sauce that is part of nearly all Thai recipes. Fish sauce is widely available in bottles in Asian markets and gourmet groceries.

TOMATILLO

Tomatillos look like small green tomatoes enclosed in paperlike husks. They are, in fact, not related to tomatoes. Tart with a fruity, fresh character, they are eaten raw and cooked and are frequently used in sauces in Mexico and in contemporary cooking in the American Southwest.

When tomatillos are ripe, their husks will have loosened a bit and will be tan. To use, twist off and discard the husk; wash the tomatillo well until it is no longer sticky. It is never necessary to peel them once the husks have been removed. One pound of tomatillos makes about 1½ cups purée. Tomatillos are readily available fresh in well-stocked produce markets. They also are available canned in the Mexican-food section of larger supermarkets.

WHITE ONION

Try to use white onions where indicated, as they have a sharper flavor than the more common yellow onion. White onions are ubiquitous in Mexican cooking. They are delicious chopped fine and used raw as a garnish for many Mexican soups.

PEPPERS

To roast and peel fresh chiles or sweet peppers, place them directly on an open flame on the burner of a gas stove. (You may want to line the burner plate with foil before beginning the roasting.) Using tongs, turn the peppers until they are blistered and charred all over, 5 to 15 minutes. Every bit of skin area must have come in contact with the flame or it simply will not peel! Proper roasting results in peppers that appear to have been cremated. They will be ashen and blackened. Fear not! There are delicious roasted peppers underneath.

If you are using an electric stove, roast the peppers on a metal rack placed over the burner; or spread the peppers on a baking sheet, position it about 3 inches from a preheated broiler, and broil for 8 to 10 minutes, turning them frequently. Do not let the peppers come into contact with an electric heating element.

Once the peppers are roasted by either of these methods, wrap them in a dry cotton towel or seal them in a plastic bag to steam for 10 minutes, or until cool enough to handle. When cool, peel off the skins; they will come off easily. Slit open and discard the stems, seeds, and veins. Try not to hold the peppers under running water during the cleaning process, as wonderful flavors get washed away.

It is important to exercise caution when handling chile peppers. Always wear rubber gloves and wash your hands carefully after touching them. Do not put your hands on your face or rub your eyes while working with peppers, as a severe burning sensation will result. It was previously thought that the pepper's seeds were responsible for the hotness. Now it is known that the placenta, or long veins that hold the seeds in place, is the culprit. Generally speaking (and there are many exceptions to this rule) the smaller the pepper the hotter it will be.

When choosing fresh peppers look for those that are smooth and unblemished. Do not purchase fresh peppers that are split or wrinkled. Fresh roasted peppers can be stored in the refrigerator for up to 3 days, or stored frozen for several months. Dried peppers are best when still pliable and bright in color or, if they have darkened, have a slight reddish hue. Very brittle, browned, or yellowed peppers should be avoided. The presence of many loose seeds in a package of dried peppers indicates age. Dried peppers should be stored in a cool, dry place, out of direct sunlight.

The varieties of peppers listed here can generally be found in well-stocked large supermarkets, Latino markets, and through mail-order sources.

ANCHO

The *ancho*, which means "wide" in Spanish, is indeed about 3 inches wide at the top, or stem end. It is the dried form of a type of *poblano* and is a warm dark red to brown. Universally used in Mexico, the pod is sweet and fruity, mild to medium-hot, and is commonly used in *mole* sauce recipes.

ANAHEIM   *See New Mexico.*

BELL

The sweet bell pepper in all its various colors—green, red, yellow, purple, chocolate—is by far the best-selling fresh pepper in the United States. It is so mild as to be downright bland. When roasted, however, it is transformed into a flavorful food. Sweet bells add sprightly color to any dish without being controversial.

CAYENNE

Commonly used in its ground, dried form, the cayenne pepper is grown for its fiery quality. It is about 4 inches long, pencil thin, and sharp at the end. Cayenne is also known as red pepper seasoning. It is generally added to foods to heat them up, in either ground or hot sauce form. In its fresh form it is used in salsas. Cayenne has a reputation for being very hot, but in reality it is less hot than many other pepper varieties.

CHILACA

This Mexican pepper is very hot in both its fresh and dried forms. Of its several varieties, the one available to us north of the border is the *negro*, and that in only its dried form, known as *pasilla negro* (q.v.). The *chilaca* pepper is very dark green and long and narrow, about 1 inch wide and 3 to 5 inches long. It is commonly used in *mole* sauce recipes.

CHIMAYÓ

Chimayó chile is a cultivar of the New Mexico chile. It is hot, bright orange, and as vivid and pure as the spectacularly beautiful valley north of Santa Fe where it is grown. It makes a wonderful, sweet and somewhat mild chile powder. Do not accept imitations. Send for it and use it, and you won't be disappointed! At Cafe Pasqual's we use it constantly.

CHIPOTLE

The brown *chipotle* chile is the dry-smoked jalapeño chile. Making its debut in the North American market recently is the *chipotle morita*, or "raspberry" *chipotle*. This *chipotle* is more pliable than other jalapeño cultivars currently on the market. It has a fruity flavor and a dark red, wrinkled appearance. *Chipotles* also are available canned in *adobo* sauce, which is a vinegared tomato-chile sauce. Watch out for the heat of the canned variety!

JALAPEÑO
In the United States the jalapeño is the next most widely grown fresh pepper after bell pepper. It is shiny and bright green and measures about 2 inches in length. The jalapeño in *escabeche*, its pickled form, is used everywhere in the country. Those nachos at the movie theater boast pickled jalapeño rings. Fresh jalapeños are medium-hot and are used often for salsas. A fairly new preparation for jalapeños is to dry them without smoke and then grind them to a powder. The resulting product is quite hot when processed this way, but adds wonderful overtones to other chiles.

MULATO
The *mulato* is the dried form of a type of *poblano*. It is very dark, almost red-black, and 3 to 5 inches long and 2½ inches wide, with sloping "shoulders." It has a rich, smoky flavor and is traditionally used in *mole* sauce recipes.

NEW MEXICO
New Mexico chiles are long and narrow, ranging in length from 4 to 10 inches. These chiles have a tangled history and need the most explanation. Early on, the name for these elongated chiles was Anaheim, after the region in southern California where they were first widely grown as a commercial crop (after being developed in New Mexico). The Anaheim chile is currently considered to be just one of the many varieties of the now, newly named pod-type called the New Mexico. What all of the New Mexico chiles have in common is that they are green when freshly picked and, if allowed to ripen on the plant, turn red. Besides the Anaheim, New Mexico chiles include the 2-inch-long Fresno, the mild Big Jim, the wildly commercially successful New Mexico No. 6-4, the medium-hot Española Improved, the Chimayó, the Dixon, and the hot Sandia varieties. Chile powder made from dried New Mexicos is often labeled *molido*.

PASILLA NEGRO
Named for its appearance (*pasilla* means "raisinlike" in Spanish), this chile is the dried form of a type of *chilaca* pepper grown in Mexico. About 5 inches long and greenish black, it is commonly used in *mole* sauce recipes.

PEQUÍN

Also spelled *piquín*, this dried red chile is quite small, about 1/2 inch wide and 3/4 of an inch long. It is very hot, so use it judiciously. It is used whole, crushed, or flaked. *Pequín* pepper may be substituted for cayenne pepper.

POBLANO

The fresh *poblano* is a dark green chile about 5 inches long and quite fleshy. It is wide at the top, tapering quickly to a blunted point. The *poblano* is excellent for stuffing. Although often thought of as a mild pepper, it can be quite hot as well. It is always used cooked. *Poblanos* are called *pasillas* in California. Do not confuse the *poblano/pasilla* with the dried *pasilla negro*.

SERRANO

The fresh *serrano* chile is dark green and from 1½ to 3 inches in length. It is nearly as popular as the jalapeño and it, too, is found pickled as well as fresh. It is much hotter than the jalapeño and is used in salsas to give real "bite" to a dish.

THAI

Used fresh, either bright green or shocking red, these thin, pointed chiles are about 1½ inches long. Because they are thin-skinned and tiny, there is no need to roast, peel, or seed them. They are used whole. These chiles are very hot—as hot or hotter than the *serrano*. Diners should be cautioned not to ingest these searing-hot devils.

Pasqual's Pantry

*T*o make many of Cafe Pasqual's recipes you will need to have the following ingredients on hand. Most of the goods can be kept on the pantry shelf for future use. Only a few require freezing.

Chiles:
- *Ancho* chiles
- Chimayó chile powder
- *Chipotle* chiles
- *Chipotle* in *adobo* (canned)
- Green chiles: roasted, frozen, dehydrated, canned
- *Mulato* chiles
- New Mexico chile powder (*molido*)
- New Mexico red chiles: dried
- *Pequín* chiles: whole, flakes

Beans:
- Black
- Pinto

Thai products:
- Fish sauce
- Kaffir lime leaves (store frozen)
- Lemongrass (store frozen if fresh is not readily available)
- Thai chiles (store frozen if fresh is not readily available)

Seeds ✤ Nuts ✤ Herbs ✤ Spices:
- Aniseeds
- Cumin seeds
- Mexican cinnamon
- Mexican oregano
- Piñon nuts
- Saffron threads
- Sesame seeds

Miscellaneous:
- Avocado leaves
- Banana leaves (store frozen)
- Kosher salt
- Lavender honey
- *Masa harina*
- Mexican chocolate
- *Posole*

Detail of wall painting entitled La Luna Se Fue a Una Fiesta *by Leovigildo Martinez.*
Depicts celebrants: upside-down man and woman. Cafe Pasqual's, Santa Fe, New Mexico.

Detail of wall painting entitled La Luna Se Fue a Una Fiesta *by Leovigildo Martinez.*
Depicts man with Cafe Pasqual's olla, or "clay pot." Cafe Pasqual's, Santa Fe, New Mexico.

GREEN CHILE SAUCE

✦

RED CHILE SAUCE

✦

BLACK BEANS

✦

PINTO BEANS

✦

REFRIED PINTO BEANS

✦

SALSA FRESCA

✦

GUACAMOLE

✦

POSOLE STEW

✦

MASA

NEW MEXICAN RECIPES

*T*he chile has been used in Mexico and in the American Southwest for at least ten thousand years. The Spanish conquerors, however, were responsible for the intense cultivation of chiles in New Mexico and played an early role in their dissemination around the world. Today, there are few cuisines that do not use the chile pepper in some form.

The chile is taken seriously in New Mexico. The vast majority of chiles produced here are grown in huge commercial operations in Hatch, located in the southern part of the state in a broad agricultural valley near Las Cruces. The acreage under commercial cultivation has more than doubled in recent years, as Americans have begun to learn more about chiles and demand has zoomed.

The New Mexico grown and processed chile has no peer. Connoisseurship of chiles is extreme here, having nearly cult proportions. Purveyors walk the fields with their growers each season to discuss and note the conditions of the year's crop. As with all matters that generate aficionados, there are debates and speculation aplenty about where the best chile is grown.

"Which chile is hottest? Red or green?" is the first question asked by the chile novice. There are no hard and fast rules defining heat. The answer depends upon the variety of the chile, the conditions under which it was grown, and the timing of the harvest. Its incendiary quality can be increased by cultivating it with limited water. In other words, a thirsty— "stressed"—plant will likely be hotter. Climate can be a factor, too. The long, hot days in southern New Mexico produce hotter chiles than those grown farther north in more temperate conditions. Also, the heat of a chile is located not in the seeds, but in the placenta of the seeds, the fleshy veins that hold the seeds in place. Natives say the Chimayó chile is mild, the Dixon chile is rich and smooth, and the Hatch chile is the hottest. Hot is not particularly important in New Mexican cooking; instead, depth of flavor and a balance between chile's piquant and fruity qualities is sought. A rule of thumb is that the wider the shoulders of the chile, the milder the flavor. (Of course, exceptions to this rule exist.) But, oh, how it varies still. My advice is to taste, taste, taste.

New Mexicans can be insufferably chauvinistic about their chiles. First of all, real chile is always spelled with an *e*, which is the proper Spanish spelling. When spelled with an *i* (Chilie or Chili), New Mexicans are talking about the Texas chile-laced dish of meat and sometimes beans, served in a bowl and dolled up with corn, olives, cheese, or whatever. It has its place, but it is not what we mean here in New Mexico when we say "chile."

A day without red or green is a day without a fix for a New Mexican. New Mexicans *need* their chiles. Green chile, when consumed, produces endorphins, that is, pain blockers, which give a sense of well-being. So it's no wonder that it feels good to eat chiles! In Santa Fe lingo, a "bowl of red" or a "bowl of green," or just a "bowl" means a cooked chile sauce made of either red or green chiles with the optional addition of meat and beans. Traditionally, pinto beans have been the expected addition to a bowl of chile. But nowadays, one is just as likely to have a "bowl" served with black beans, a custom started by Cafe Pasqual's many years ago and now practiced widely throughout Santa Fe.

New Mexico–style chile is *not* a condiment, not meant to enhance, as with a dab of salsa. New Mexican chile is a sauce meant to enrobe enchiladas, burritos, soft tacos, and *huevos rancheros* lavishly. Our chile sauces are made from either fresh-roasted green chiles or from dried red chile pods. The dried pods may be either rehydrated, blended, and then sieved to make a sauce, or the pods may be ground to a powder and transformed into a sauce by adding the powder to a roux of oil and flour.

If you cannot obtain New Mexico chiles, substitute fresh *poblano* chiles or the New Mexico variety from California called the Anaheim, or send for the frozen product (see Mail-Order Sources). If you must use a canned product, the least preferable choice, be sure to rinse it well with water. It will be mushy in texture and not optimum in flavor. Do not confuse New Mexico chiles with pickled jalapeños, *serranos*, or green bell peppers. Green bell peppers have absolutely no "heat" and are not a substitute for fresh green chiles. If New Mexico chile powder is unavailable, use ground *ancho* chile in its place. Avoid using red chile powder that has been mixed with spices. Look for chile powders labeled "pure."

The diversity of New Mexican chile recipes is astounding. The range includes the addition of shredded pork, pork in chunks, chicken, or hand-chopped beef. Game is often used in red chile sauces in our region. Chile sauce comes in every color, from the bright orange of Chimayó to the rich red brown derived from the chiles in Dixon, which is located in the northern part of the state.

Red chiles drying for winter use on a well-house roof in the Velarde Valley in New Mexico.

Because of New Mexico's one-crop climate, chile harvest time is the only time of year when you can get fresh green chiles in quantity. A drive through the small valleys to Taos, either by the high road that winds through the tiny village of Chimayó or the low road that parallels the Rio Grande, stopping at the roadside stands, offers ample opportunity to buy fresh chiles by the bagful.

At harvest time the fresh, bright red chiles, those that have been left on the chile plant to mature, are gathered up and strung together with stout cotton cord to form *ristras*, or "ropes" of chiles two to eight feet long, to be hung outside to dry in the sunlight, generally under a roof overhang or in the shelter of a porch. In this form, they are ready for storage. Because of the low humidity of our high-desert region, drying is the traditional method of storing red chiles for use during the long, cold New Mexican winter. Alternatively, loose red chile pods are spread on the sloped tin roofs of the farmhouses to dry in the bright autumnal sun, then stored in bulk.

Green chile pods have a different commercial fate. At harvest time, entrepreneurs set up giant steel tumbler drums, often in supermarket parking lots, to roast the chiles by the burlap bagfuls. The propane-fueled flames char the skin of the chiles to make them easy to peel and, in the process, caramelize the fruits to bring out the flavors. Shoppers rush the chiles home to be peeled and put up in small plastic bags, then frozen for use throughout the year until the next harvest.

Chiles from Mexico are used for both traditional and contemporary Southwest cooking. At Pasqual's, and in the following recipes, you will encounter the *ancho, mulato, chipotle, pasilla negro,* and *pequín* chiles, all of which are imported from Mexico in dried form. These Mexican chiles are filled with surprises and wonders for the cook, but are not so generally available north of the border.

There are nearly 200 different varieties of chiles. Add to that the fact that many varieties go by more than one name, depending upon the region. You will have a less confusing time of it if you learn to identify chiles by their physical appearance and taste, in addition to their name. Understanding chiles and appreciating them in their diversity is a lifelong undertaking, but what a delicious and stimulating life study. And since growing chiles yourself is really quite easy, the study can begin in your own backyard. Be adventurous! And while you're at it, plant some corn.

Here in the Southwest, corn is sacred to the Native Americans, who revere it and regard it as the Mother. The cycle of corn is the cycle of life, and many ritual dances are based on it. The dry farming methods used today by the natives of North America for the cultivation of their life-sustaining crops are the same that have been used for millennia.

Corn goes by the name maize as well. When the native people discovered Columbus on their shores, they brought him gifts of tobacco and maize. The custom of the English, however, was to refer to the staple grain of any country as the country's corn. For instance, if rye was the staple grain, then rye was automatically called the corn. Thus, when English-speaking immigrants arrived in North America, they called the maize being cultivated here corn.

Nutritional studies show that corn is low in tryptophan and lysine, which are amino acids that help in the absorption of niacin and in its manufacture. Additionally, corn's niacin content is molecularly bound and can only be released for use by the human body through alkaline processing. Corn must be eaten in combination with protein-rich or niacin-releasing foods, such as beans, which supplement its deficiencies.

In his journal, Columbus noted that the native people always planted corn in association with beans. I find it fascinating that this health-conscious partnering was known to Native Americans long before the arrival of the first European settlers, centuries before the advent of nutritional studies. Indeed, account after account attest to the astute planting methods of the Native Americans, including the fact that the corn formed a natural trellis around which the bean vines could twine.

In this chapter, you will find recipes that are at the heart of New Mexican cuisine. Many of them are essential to the preparation of the regional dishes that appear throughout the book.

GREEN CHILE SAUCE

*T*his is the sauce we use to dress omelets, *huevos motuleños* (page 51), *huevos rancheros* (page 53), enchiladas, and burritos. Called *chile verde*, it is the gravy of New Mexico. Gravies are the personal mark of a cook, so please feel free to make this recipe yours with your own additions or deletions.

Green chiles are available fresh, frozen, canned, or dried. If using fresh chiles for this recipe, which are preferred, make a special effort to obtain New Mexico green chiles rather than use the milder, ubiquitous Anaheim variety. If New Mexico green chiles are unavailable, substitute fresh *poblano* chiles. *Poblano* chiles are shiny, dark green, and have more of a bell pepper shape than the longer, pointed New Mexico and Anaheim varieties. Fresh chiles need to be roasted, peeled, stemmed, seeded, and chopped before using. Frozen chiles have already been prepared in this manner. If using canned chiles, the least preferable choice, rinse them thoroughly before using. Canned and frozen chile products are specifically labeled by the processor as to whether the chiles are hot, medium-hot, or mild. If using dried green chiles, soak in hot water to cover for 45 minutes to rehydrate them, then drain, seed, and chop.

Makes about 3½ cups

About 1½ pounds fresh mild green New Mexico chiles, roasted, peeled, seeded, deveined, and chopped to measure 2 cups (page 22)

About 3/4 pound fresh hot green New Mexico chiles, roasted, peeled, seeded, deveined, and chopped to measure 1 cup (page 22)

4 cups water

1/2 white onion, cut into medium dice

2 teaspoons dried Mexican oregano or marjoram leaves

6 cloves garlic, finely minced

1½ teaspoons kosher salt

2 tablespoons vegetable oil

3 tablespoons all-purpose flour

Place all the ingredients, except the vegetable oil and flour, in a large saucepan over medium heat. Simmer, uncovered, until juice has thickened and is opaque, 20 to 30 minutes. Stir occasionally, taking care that the chiles do not burn or stick to the bottom of the pan.

In a small bowl, whisk together the oil and flour until smooth and well blended, to form the base for a roux. Place in a saucepan over medium-high heat until hot and bubbling. Reduce the heat to low and whisk constantly until the roux is slightly brown and has a nutty flavor. Remove from the heat. ≈

Add 1/2 cup of the green chile mixture to the roux and whisk thoroughly until smooth. Add the roux to the remaining chile mixture and cook over low heat until the sauce thickens and the "flour taste" disappears, about 15 minutes. Adjust to taste with salt.

Remove from the heat, let cool, cover, and store in a nonreactive container in the refrigerator until needed. The sauce may be refrigerated for up to 4 days. Check it for sourness if held any longer. The sauce may be frozen for up to 2 months. To heat the sauce for serving, place it in a nonreactive pan over medium-low heat, stirring frequently to prevent scorching.

❖ *Variation with meat* (con carne): *Prepare the sauce as directed. Cut 1 pound pork shoulder in half and trim off any fat. Place the pork in a saucepan and add 2 white onions, quartered; 1½ teaspoons salt; 2 teaspoons cumin seeds; 2 teaspoons dried Mexican oregano leaves; 12 whole black peppercorns, and water to cover (about 8 cups). Bring to a boil and skim off and discard the resulting foam. Cover and simmer over low heat until the meat is tender, about 1 hour. Drain and, with two opposing forks, shred the meat into long strings. Chop the shredded meat with a cleaver into 1/2-inch lengths and stir into the finished chile sauce.*

RED CHILE SAUCE

Since I strongly prefer red chile sauce, or *chile colorado*, made from whole, dried red New Mexico chile pods, it is the only way we prepare it at Pasqual's. Some prefer to use a *molido* (ground chile) and roux mixture, but I think the fruity flavors of the chile are lost when a powder is used. The debate between proponents of the whole and the powdered forms is a serious matter of personal taste. There are armed camps on this subject!

Be sure not to touch your hands to your eyes or face while handling the chiles! The fiery quality of the chile is real, and will burn sensitive skin. Wash your hands well after preparing chiles. It is best to wear rubber gloves throughout the process.

Makes about 4 cups

60 dried red New Mexico chiles, about 3/4 pound or 8 cups packed, rinsed, stemmed, and seeded

1 white onion, coarsely chopped

8 cloves garlic

2 teaspoons dried Mexican oregano leaves

2 teaspoons kosher salt

1 teaspoon ground cumin

To rehydrate the chiles, place them in a nonreactive 8-quart stockpot and add hot tap water to cover. The chiles will float, so cover them with a plate slightly smaller than the circumference of the pot to keep them submerged. Let soak until soft and pliable, about 20 minutes. The fumes released during this process are fairly intense and you may experience some difficulty in breathing. Fling open the windows and kitchen door.

When the chiles are fully rehydrated, remove the plate and add all the remaining ingredients to the pot. Bring to a boil over high heat, reduce the heat to low, and simmer, uncovered, for 20 minutes.

Drain the chiles, reserving the liquid. Working in batches, place the chiles in a blender, filling it about three-fourths full. Add about 1/2 cup of the reserved liquid and blend the contents to a thick catsuplike consistency. (You may need to adjust the amount of liquid you add.)

When the sauce is thoroughly blended, pass it through a fine-mesh strainer. We use a china cap (see note) with 1/8-inch holes to remove unblended chiles and any seeds. The finished chile sauce should be smooth and thick. Repeat until all the chiles are used. Adjust to taste with salt. Processing the sauce is a messy job. Be careful because red chile may permanently stain clothing, countertops, and cutting boards.

The sauce may be stored in a nonreactive container in the refrigerator for up to 4 days. Check it for sourness if held any longer. The sauce may be frozen for up to 2 months. To heat the sauce for serving, place in a nonreactive pan over medium-low heat, stirring frequently to prevent scorching.

Chile pickers resting at day's end. Chile harvest near Hatch, New Mexico.

Note: A china cap is a cone-shaped strainer and is a good addition to any kitchen.

❖ Variation with meat (con carne): See the variation with meat for Green Chile Sauce on page 35 and follow the same directions.

BLACK BEANS

*B*lack beans, also known as turtle beans, are native to Central and South America. I prefer them to the Southwest's more traditional pinto; they have more flavor and seem to be more easily digested. They also do not need the addition of meat fat for flavor the way pinto beans do.

Do not soak these beans overnight. Presoaking actually seems to lengthen the cooking time. Also, to achieve soft, tender beans, do not add salt until the end of the cooking process. Adding salt early in the cooking will make the beans tough.

Makes about 4 cups; serves 6 to 10

2½ cups (about 1¼ pounds) dried
    black beans

1/2 white onion, finely diced

1/2 green or red bell pepper, seeded,
    deveined, and finely diced

2 fresh jalapeño chiles, stemmed,
    seeded, and minced

1/2 teaspoon ground cumin

1/2 bay leaf

3 quarts water

1 teaspoon salt, or to taste

Sort the beans by hand to remove small rocks and bits of organic debris, and clean thoroughly, rinsing under running water.

Combine all the ingredients, except the salt, in a stockpot. Bring to a boil and then reduce the heat to low. Simmer, uncovered, until the beans are soft, about 1½ hours. Add water as needed to keep the beans immersed during cooking. When the beans are properly cooked, they are tender but their skins remain unbroken.

Season with the salt. Cool the beans and store in their liquid to cover in the refrigerator. The beans will keep for up to 5 days in a container with a tight-fitting lid. You may freeze the beans for up to 2 months. When thawed they will be softer in texture.

❖ *Variations: Halfway through the cooking, add to the beans 2 lemons, sliced, seeded, and coarsely chopped; and/or 1½ teaspoons medium-hot New Mexico red chile powder (molido) and any leftover salsa. For more piquant beans, add 1 fresh serrano chile, stemmed, seeded, and finely chopped.*

Pinto Beans

*T*hese are the traditional beans of the three cultures of New Mexico—Native American, Hispano, and Anglo. *Pinto* means "painted" in Spanish. Dabs of brown mottle the beans, but disappear during cooking. The pinto is rich in nutritional value and, consequently, has been vital to this high-desert region for centuries. Because of the long cooking time, you may wish to use the canned product. If you do, you will need to "help" the flavor by sprinkling chopped white onion on top, either raw or sautéed with chile powder, as in Refried Pinto Beans (page 40). Try stirring in a bit of minced fresh jalapeño or *serrano* chile or whatever you fancy to add interest.

Makes about 4 cups; serves 6 to 10

2¹/₂ cups (about 1 pound) dried pinto beans

2 tablespoons bacon drippings (optional)

2 cloves garlic, finely chopped

3 quarts water

2 teaspoons salt, or to taste

Sort the pintos by hand to remove small rocks and bits of organic debris, and clean thoroughly, rinsing under running water.

Combine all the ingredients, except the salt, in a stockpot. Cover and bring to a boil. Reduce the heat to low and simmer until tender, about 2¹/₂ hours. Add water as needed to keep the water level 2 inches above the beans at all times. The beans should be soft but their skins should remain unbroken. Add the salt during the last 30 minutes of cooking.

Cool the beans and store in their liquid in the refrigerator in a container with a tight-fitting lid for up to 5 days. The beans may be frozen for up to 2 months.

REFRIED PINTO BEANS

*S*erve these *frijoles refritos* as a side dish or as a dip for corn tortilla chips, or spread them on a tostada, top with shredded Monterey Jack cheese, shredded lettuce, and Tomatillo-Cilantro Salsa (page 104–5) or *Salsa Fresca* (page 41) and serve as a lunch dish.

Makes about 2½ cups; serves 4 to 6 as a side dish

3 tablespoons bacon drippings or
    vegetable oil

1/2 yellow onion, finely diced

2 teaspoons Chimayó chile powder or
    New Mexico medium-hot red chile
    powder (*molido*; optional)

2 cups Pinto Beans, including about
    2/3 cup cooking liquid (page 39)

1/2 cup grated Monterey Jack cheese

Place a cast-iron skillet over medium heat and add the bacon drippings or oil. Add the onion and sauté until translucent, about 4 minutes. Add the chile powder and continue to sauté for another 2 minutes.

Add the pinto beans and their cooking liquid. Crush the beans with the back of a wooden spoon or a potato masher until a mash consisting mostly of crushed beans is achieved. Leave some beans whole to give the mash an appetizing texture.

Continue to cook until heated through, stirring frequently to prevent the beans from scorching. Top with the cheese and serve.

SALSA FRESCA

*I*n American culinary history, 1992 will be remembered as the year salsa outsold catsup to become the nation's number one condiment. That's terrific news to me because it's a healthy step away from the role of sugar as a palate pleaser into the fascinating world of chile flavors.

Every morning at Cafe Pasqual's we prepare by hand four gallons of this essential salsa. We serve it as an accompaniment to our breakfast and lunch quesadillas. It is full of fresh flavor, has crunch, and the "heat" can easily be turned up or down. We use vine-ripened tomatoes at the height of summer when they are plentiful. Otherwise, Italian plum (Roma) tomatoes are available year-round and are superior to other commercial tomatoes.

Always make salsa by hand using a good sharp knife. A machine reduces the ingredients to a mushy liquid and, at that point, you might as well buy a jar of commercial salsa.

Makes about 2 cups

10 ounces Italian plum tomatoes (about 5)

1/4 white onion

1/2 fresh *serrano* chile or 1 fresh jalapeño chile, stemmed, seeded, and finely minced

1/4 cup fresh cilantro (coriander) leaves and some stems, chopped

1/4 teaspoon salt, or to taste

Small pinch of ground cumin (optional)

Chop the tomatoes by hand. To create a perfect 1/8-inch dice, slice off the stem end and stand the tomato on its now-flat surface. Slice straight down to make 1/8-inch-wide slabs. Turn the tomato on its side, keeping the slices together and removing one side piece to make a flat surface. Cut 1/8-inch lengths, creating strips. Turn the cut tomato as a unit and cut across the tomato in 1/8-inch increments, creating a dice. Cut the reserved slice into dice as well. Put the diced tomatoes into a nonreactive bowl.

Cut the onion in the same-size dice as the tomatoes and put in the bowl with the tomatoes.

Add the chile and cilantro. Add the salt and a very small amount of cumin, if you like. Stir well.

Note: Because the piquant qualities of onions and chiles vary, you may need to adjust one or the other of these ingredients to taste. Serve the salsa at room temperature within a few hours of preparing it. It does not store well; the tomatoes and onion become soft and the flavors dissipate.

GUACAMOLE

*I*n the Southwest, guacamole is always in demand. Indeed, all of America is now aware of this classic *mole*. At Cafe Pasqual's we serve it as a topping on burritos and as a filling in quesadillas and omelets. But it is also wonderful served simply as a dip for yellow corn tortilla chips or raw vegetables such as jicama, bell pepper, or celery strips.

Superb guacamole depends on perfectly ripe and flavorful ingredients. Undoubtedly, you will have to make adjustments for the condition of the available avocados and tomatoes. Avocados are ripe when they yield to gentle fingertip pressure. The black, bumpy-skinned Haas variety is preferred because of its rich flavor. In winter, the smooth-skinned Fuertes avocado from Florida is widely available, but it is difficult to make great guacamole from it. If you must use the Fuertes variety, add extra lime juice, a bit of olive oil to offset its watery nature, and use the ripest Italian plum tomatoes you can find.

Guacamole should be mixed using only hand implements. An old-fashioned hand-held potato masher works well, leaving appetizing little chunks of avocado, tomato, and onion to please the tastebuds.

Makes about 3 cups

3 large, fully ripe avocados, peeled and pitted

1 tomato, seeded and finely diced

1/3 white onion, finely diced

1 fresh jalapeño chile or 1/2 fresh *serrano* chile, stemmed, seeded and finely minced (optional)

3 cloves garlic, finely minced

Salt

Freshly ground black pepper (optional)

Juice of 3 limes or 2 lemons

In a large bowl, mash the avocados with a fork, potato masher, or other hand implement until the mixture is generally smooth, but with some chunks left for texture.

Add the tomato, onion, and the chile, if using, and mix thoroughly. Season with the garlic and with salt and black pepper (if used) to taste. Use a mortar and pestle, if you have one, to blend these seasoning ingredients before adding them. Add the lime or lemon juice and mix well.

Serve the guacamole within 2 hours of preparing it. To store guacamole, press plastic wrap directly onto its surface, to prevent the discoloration that occurs from contact with air, and place in the refrigerator. Serve at room temperature.

POSOLE STEW

*P*osole is a celebratory dish. It is meant to feed crowds of family and friends. This hearty corn stew is the traditional Christmas and feasting meal in New Mexico for both the pueblo Indians and the Hispanos. Eat *posole* on New Year's Day for good luck all year long!

In addition to being the name for the stew, *posole* is also the term for white field corn, known as *cacahuazincle*, that has been processed with slaked lime to remove its hard outer husk. Although the corn is similar to hominy, canned hominy cannot be substituted for it. Dried *posole* takes some five hours to cook; fresh-frozen *posole* takes two to three hours. A big pot of this popular regional stew is redolent with chiles and garlic and often includes succulent pieces of pork shoulder. The *posole* recipe offered here uses pork as an ingredient, but it is equally delicious made without meat.

Serve the stew as a main course with garnishes of sliced radish, avocado chunks, lime wedges, or tortilla strips on the side, to be added as the diner desires. *Posole* may be served without garnish as a side dish to other regional specialties. Leftovers can be refrigerated for up to six days, or frozen for up to two months.

Serves 6 to 8 as a main course, or 10 to 12 as a side dish

2 packages (3/4 pound each) dried *posole* or fresh-frozen *posole*

10 ounces pork shoulder, trimmed of fat and cut into 1-inch cubes (optional)

2 cups Green Chile Sauce (pages 34–35)

6 cloves garlic, or more to taste, finely minced

1 white onion, finely diced

4 dried red New Mexico chiles, or more to taste, rinsed, stemmed, seeded, and coarsely chopped

2 tablespoons Chimayó chile powder

2 teaspoons ground cumin

1 tablespoon dried Mexican oregano leaves

1 tablespoon red pepper flakes or *pequín* chile flakes

2 teaspoons kosher salt, or to taste

6 quarts water

If using fresh-frozen *posole*, rinse it well under cold running water. Place all of the ingredients in a large pot and bring to a boil. Reduce the heat to low and simmer, uncovered, stirring occasionally, until the kernels have opened up and are tender, 2½ to 5 hours, depending upon the type of *posole* you are using. Add water as needed to keep the *posole* just covered with liquid. When the stew is ready, the consistency should be that of a thick soup.

Adjust to taste with more garlic, dried red chile, and salt before serving.

Squash- and cornfields, Gallina Canyon Ranch, north of Abiquiu, New Mexico.

MASA

*M*asa is Spanish for "dough." It refers specifically to the corn dough that is used for making tortillas, tamales, and other cooked, thick corn-dough dishes.

To make *masa* one has to begin with white field corn. This particular variety has a hard husk around each kernel. The kernels are first soaked in a slaked lime solution to soften the husk, the husk is discarded, and then the corn is rinsed at least half a dozen times. The resulting *nixtamal* is ground into *masa*, flavored with spices, shortening, and salt, and patted into tortillas, tamales, or any manner of corn-based dishes. The recipe for making *nixtamal* is quite lengthy and labor-intensive and not given here. This recipe uses *masa harina*.

Dehydrated *nixtamal* is called *masa harina*, or "cornmeal flour." It does not have the intense corn flavors of the wet *nixtamal*, but it is widely available in supermarkets in the flour section. If a selection of grinds is available, choose coarse ground. (*Masa trigo* is wheat-based flour and is used for making flour tortillas.) For more authentic flavor, use lard in place of the vegetable shortening.

Makes about 3 cups, enough dough for 12 to 14 tamales; serves 6 or 7

3 cups masa harina

1 teaspoon baking powder

1 teaspoon ground cumin

1 ½ teaspoons salt

1 cup solid vegetable shortening, at room temperature

2 cups water

Combine the *masa harina*, baking powder, cumin, and salt in a large bowl. In a separate bowl, beat the shortening by hand or use an electric mixer, the preferred method, until softened, about 3 minutes on high speed. Add the dry mixture to the shortening and beat on medium speed until well mixed, about 2 minutes. Add the water gradually and mix on medium speed until a smooth and soft claylike texture is achieved, about 3 minutes. You may need to add more water to arrive at the right consistency because the moisture content of commercial *masa harina* varies.

Use the *masa* immediately.

Chorizo Burrito

✦

Huevos Motuleños

✦

Breakfast Quesadillas

✦

Huevos Rancheros

✦

Griddled Polenta with Chorizo, Corn,
and Red Chile Sauce

✦

Maga's Blintzes

✦

Mexican Hot Chocolate

✦

Chorizo Sausage

BREAKFAST

When you eat at Cafe Pasqual's you understand that we place as high a value on the quality of our food at its source and its preparation as on the presentation. These high standards start right at breakfast time! We are known for our breakfasts. We use real eggs, real butter, and real potatoes. We use nothing frozen or commercially prepared. The sausages are made in-house, as is the bread for the toast.

I have always known that the great cafes of the world respect breakfast. At Cafe Pasqual's we serve this beloved meal all day. Even after the lunch menu is added at eleven o'clock, customers can still get corned beef hash and eggs, *huevos motuleños*, grilled trout with home-fried potatoes, or quesadillas filled with bacon and eggs. If you feel like breakfast at two o'clock in the afternoon, so be it. Sadly, we've lost cooks over this policy. It puts a huge strain on the kitchen to produce two menus at once, but breakfast-food lovers do not obey the clock.

Cooking breakfast is an art. Eggs require skill to prepare them properly. They are mostly protein, and protein gets rubbery very quickly if cooked improperly. Luckily, our breakfast chef, Rudy Gabaldon, has a gentle way with an egg pan. He can deftly turn out 450 perfectly cooked brunches in 360 minutes!

Some of Gabaldon's trade secrets? He uses a seven-inch nonstick sauté pan. It is terrific for eggs. It heats evenly and the eggs don't stick. And when Rudy cooks an egg, he uses neither heat that is too high, nor is he overly cautious. He employs rubber spatulas to "tend" the eggs, to stir the scramble, or to lift the edge of an omelet. And he flip eggs, he never turns them. Teach yourself to do this. Slightly thrust the pan out and away from you and quickly bring it back to catch the egg that has been thrown upward. You may have ten or twenty disasters, but you'll get it. This method of flipping keeps eggs from breaking or falling out of the pan, eliminates the awkward handling of implements, and, perhaps most importantly, prevents swearing and fury in the kitchen. A final secret of chef Gabaldon is to beat the eggs vigorously for a scramble or omelet at least twenty times with the tines of a table fork. This ensures that all of the egg is well incorporated for a perfectly cooked dish.

Always be sure your breakfast ingredients are the freshest and best available and warm the serving plates. There is nothing worse than cold eggs. Also, coordinate the preparations so that everyone is fed at the same time, including the cook! No one should miss out on the table conversation over a delicious, carefully prepared breakfast or brunch.

CHORIZO BURRITO

Mexican chorizo is sausage made with pork, chile powder, chile flakes, spices, and herbs. It is quite different from Spanish chorizo, so be sure to specify the Mexican type when purchasing the sausage. It is now widely available from better markets, but the commercial sausage is inferior to what you can easily make in your own food processor (pages 60–61). Make it in quantity and freeze it in practical portion sizes. If you end up purchasing the chorizo in link form, remove the casings and handle it as if it were bulk sausage.

We offer this very popular burrito at breakfast, but it is requested and served at lunch as well. Chef Gus Macias, a native Santa Fean, made the prototype for this remarkable dish. This is a lot of burrito, so make sure your diners are hungry, or adjust the recipe for smaller portions.

Serves 6

For the panfried potatoes:

6 red potatoes

1/2 to 3/4 cup clarified unsalted butter

6 cups Red Chile Sauce (pages 36–37) or Green Chile Sauce (pages 34–35), or 3 cups of each sauce

2 tablespoons clarified butter

1 cup plus 2 tablespoons thinly sliced scallions, including the green tops

3/4 pound Mexican Chorizo Sausage, crumbled (pages 60–61)

12 eggs, beaten

6 white-flour or whole-wheat tortillas

1½ cups shredded Monterey Jack cheese

To make the panfried potatoes, place the potatoes in a saucepan and add cold water to cover. Bring to a boil and boil until potatoes are easily pierced with the tines of a fork, 25 to 35 minutes. Drain and let cool completely. (The potatoes may be cooled and stored overnight at this point.) Slice into 1/8-inch-thick rounds.

Melt half of the butter in a cast-iron skillet over high heat. When the butter begins to sizzle, add half of the potatoes and cook, turning once, until golden brown, about 15 minutes' total cooking time. Remove to paper towels to drain. Repeat with the remaining potatoes. Set aside until ready to assemble the burritos.

Preheat a broiler. Place the chile sauce(s) in saucepan(s) over medium-low heat and heat to serving temperature, stirring frequently to prevent scorching.

Heat the butter in a large sauté pan over high heat. When the butter begins to sizzle, add the 1 cup scallions and all of the chorizo. Fry until the chorizo is cooked through, about 3 minutes. Add the eggs and stir frequently with a rubber spatula until the eggs are cooked to the desired doneness. Remove from the heat.

≈

To assemble each burrito, place a tortilla on a flameproof serving plate. Place one sixth of the egg mixture and one sixth of the panfried potatoes (about 2/3 cup) in the center of the tortilla. Roll up the tortilla and place seam side down on the plate.

Pour 1 cup of the chile sauce over each burrito and sprinkle with 1/4 cup of the cheese. Run under the broiler until the cheese is bubbly. Garnish each serving with 1 teaspoon of the remaining scallions. Serve immediately.

Huevos Motuleños

*T*he village of Motul on Mexico's Yucatán peninsula is the origin of this wonderful concoction. In Motul, cooks serve this dish with diced ham, but we have always been satisfied with it as a vegetarian offering. The fried bananas are what "make" it.

Serves 4

2 cups Black Beans (page 38)

4 cups Green Chile Sauce (pages 34–35)

8 blue corn tortillas

3 or 4 tablespoons vegetable oil

1/4 cup plus 2 tablespoons clarified butter

4 bananas, peeled and split in half lengthwise

8 eggs

1 cup crumbled feta cheese

1 cup fresh shelled or frozen green peas, cooked until just tender in boiling water, well drained, and kept hot

2 cups *Salsa Fresca* (page 41)

8 fresh cilantro (coriander) sprigs for garnish

Place the beans and chile sauce in separate saucepans over medium-low heat and heat to serving temperature, stirring frequently to prevent scorching.

Brush each tortilla on both sides with vegetable oil. Place a dry skillet over high heat. When the pan is hot, add the tortillas, one at a time, and heat, turning once, until soft, about 5 seconds on each side. Set aside.

In a sauté pan, melt the 1/4 cup butter over medium-high heat. When the butter sizzles, add the banana halves and cook, turning once, until golden brown on both sides, about 5 minutes on each side. Set aside.

In another sauté pan, melt the 2 tablespoons butter and cook the eggs as desired: fried, over easy, sunny side up, or scrambled.

To assemble the *motuleños*, place 2 tortillas side by side on each serving plate. Spoon 1/2 cup of the beans into the center of each tortilla, and place 2 fried eggs or one fourth of the scrambled eggs on top of the beans. Ladle the chile sauce around the eggs, covering the beans. Scatter 1/4 cup of the cheese and 1/4 cup of the peas over each serving. Top with 1/2 cup of the salsa, and place 2 fried banana halves along either side of each serving. Garnish with cilantro sprigs. Serve immediately.

BREAKFAST QUESADILLAS

*B*reakfast quesadillas are a New Mexican specialty. More often than not, residents begin their day with their bacon and eggs wrapped in a tortilla. Here is our version of that breakfast. We use thickly cut apple-smoked bacon, fresh country eggs, and flavorful guacamole. If you can't find the apple-smoked bacon, ask your market to special order it. At Cafe Pasqual's we offer our customers the choice of no-cholesterol eggs (available in the frozen-food section of well-stocked supermarkets). Be sure to serve this meal with the fresh salsa for a piquant balance to the rich ingredients.

Serves 4

8 eggs

7 tablespoons clarified butter

8 whole-wheat tortillas

16 thick slices apple-smoked bacon,
   fried and kept warm

1 cup Guacamole (page 42)

2 cups *Salsa Fresca* (page 41)

8 fresh cilantro (coriander) or flat-leaf
   parsley sprigs for garnish

Preheat an oven to 250° F.

To prepare the scrambled eggs, place the eggs in a bowl and whisk them vigorously until completely blended. Set aside. In a nonstick sauté pan over medium heat, melt 4 tablespoons of the butter. When the butter sizzles, add the eggs and lower the heat, if necessary, to cook them gently to the desired doneness. Set aside and keep warm.

Meanwhile, in another skillet or on a griddle over medium-high heat, melt the remaining 3 tablespoons butter. When the butter sizzles, slip a tortilla onto the hot surface. Cook for 2 minutes and turn the tortilla over. Place one-eighth of the scrambled eggs, two strips of bacon, and 2 tablespoons of the guacamole in the middle of the tortilla. Fold the tortilla in half to form a quesadilla. Cook 1 more minute to crisp the outside of the quesadilla, then remove from the heat and keep warm in the oven. Repeat with the remaining ingredients.

Place 2 quesadillas on each serving plate. Top with the salsa and 2 cilantro or parsley sprigs.

HUEVOS RANCHEROS

Our *huevos rancheros* are thick with chile sauce and cheese, unlike most versions I've had elsewhere. *Huevos rancheros* are the preferred breakfast on the working cattle ranches in Mexico, so have a big day planned for this hearty beginning!

Serves 4

4 cups Black Beans (page 38) or Pinto Beans (page 39)

4 cups Red Chile Sauce (pages 36-37) or Green Chile Sauce (pages 34-35), or 2 cups of each sauce

4 blue corn or whole-wheat or white-flour tortillas, plus 4 whole-wheat tortillas for serving

2 tablespoons vegetable oil, if using corn tortillas

2 tablespoons clarified butter

8 eggs

3 cups grated Monterey Jack cheese

1/2 cup finely sliced scallions for garnish

Preheat a broiler. Place the beans and chile sauce(s) in separate saucepans over medium-low heat and heat to serving temperature, stirring frequently to prevent scorching.

If using blue corn tortillas, brush each tortilla on both sides with vegetable oil. Place a dry skillet over high heat. When the pan is hot, add the tortillas, one at a time, and heat, turning once, until soft, about 5 seconds on each side. If using flour tortillas, this step is unnecessary.

In a sauté pan melt the butter and cook the eggs as desired: fried, over easy, sunny side up, or scrambled.

Place a corn or wheat tortilla on each of 4 flame-proof serving plates. Spoon 1 cup of the beans over each tortilla and top with the eggs, placed in the center. Ladle 1 cup of the chile sauce over each serving. Sprinkle the cheese over all. Slip under the broiler until the cheese melts and bubbles, just a few minutes. Garnish with the scallions and serve piping hot. Accompany with a warmed whole-wheat tortilla for each person.

Griddled Polenta with Chorizo, Corn, and Red Chile Sauce

I am a confessed polenta addict. I love cornmeal at any meal, but somehow polenta, the Italian treatment of cornmeal, belongs at breakfast. I created this bowl of breakfast polenta with texture in mind. I like how the different components interact with one another—and the intense colors are stunning in combination. Do use the soft Italian *mascarpone* cheese the recipe calls for, as it lends an incomparable richness and smoothness to the yellow wonder. This recipe is less complicated if all the elements are prepared in advance of the final assembly.

Serves 6

For the green chile polenta:

6 cups water

2 teaspoons salt

2 cups polenta

2 eggs

1 tablespoon olive oil

About 1/2 pound fresh New Mexico, Anaheim or *poblano* chiles, roasted, peeled, seeded, and chopped to measure 3/4 cup (page 22)

1/2 cup freshly grated Parmesan cheese

1/2 cup *mascarpone* cheese

1 tablespoon butter

3 cups Red Chile Sauce (pages 36–37)

3/4 cup clarified butter

1 pound Chorizo Sausage (pages 60–61)

3 cups fresh or frozen corn kernels, cooked until barely tender in boiling water, well drained, and kept hot

12 fresh cilantro (coriander) sprigs for garnish

To prepare the polenta, in a heavy-bottomed saucepan, bring the water to a boil and add the salt. Reduce the heat so the water is at a rolling boil and slowly add the polenta, stirring constantly with a wooden spoon. Cook over medium heat for 10 to 15 minutes, stirring frequently. The polenta should be quite stiff and will noticeably change taste from "raw" to "cooked." It will appear to "tear" away from the sides of the pan at this point.

Remove from the heat and transfer the polenta to a bowl. Using an electric mixer fitted with the paddle attachment and set on high speed, or using a wooden spoon and working by hand, add the eggs, one at a time, beating well after each addition. Add the olive oil and continue to beat for 3 minutes. Add the chiles and Parmesan and *mascarpone* cheeses and mix thoroughly. Adjust to taste with salt. ≈

Use the butter to grease a jelly-roll sheet pan measuring 13 by 18 by 1 inch (or a baking sheet with sides measuring 11 by 16 by 1/2 inch). Pour the polenta into the pan. Dampen your hands with water and pat the polenta to achieve a flat, even surface. Cover with plastic wrap and refrigerate until cool and set. (At this point the polenta may be stored in the refrigerator for a day in advance of serving.)

Cut the set polenta into 6 equal squares. Then cut the squares in half on the diagonal to make 12 triangles.

Place the chile sauce in a saucepan over medium-low heat and heat to serving temperature, stirring frequently to prevent scorching.

Melt the clarified butter in a griddle or cast-iron skillet over medium-high heat. Add the polenta triangles and fry, turning once, until golden brown on both sides, about 5 minutes on each side.

Meanwhile, crumble the chorizo into a sauté pan over medium-high heat. Cook, stirring, until browned, about 4 to 6 minutes.

To serve, place 2 polenta triangles on each serving plate. Top with the chorizo and the corn. Ladle 1/2 cup of the chile sauce over each serving and garnish with the cilantro.

MAGA'S BLINTZES

My grandmother Maga, also known as Jenny Kagel, was a great Old World cook. She spoiled our family by making these extravagantly luscious brunch favorites weekly. A big department-store box of blintzes was invariably ready for us to take home from our visits with her. The blintzes were laid out in neat rows of uniform, perfectly folded stuffed crêpes, butter yellow and dotted with golden spots. *Always* serve these with sour cream and strawberry jam. It's a tradition worth upholding.

Makes 18 blintzes; serves 6

For the crêpes:

3 eggs

2 cups low-fat milk (2 %)

1 1/2 cups all-purpose flour

1/2 cup clarified unsalted butter, melted

For the filling:

2 3/4 cups cottage cheese

1/2 cup fine dried bread crumbs, from a good French loaf

3/4 cup clarified unsalted butter

For the topping:

2 cups sour cream

1 cup strawberry jam

To prepare the crêpe batter, put the eggs, milk, and flour into a blender or a food processor with the steel blade. Blend on high speed until all the ingredients are incorporated, 1 to 2 minutes.

To cook the crêpes, heat a 7-inch nonstick sauté pan until very hot. When hot, brush the pan with a little of the melted butter, using a total of 1/2 cup butter to cook all the crêpes. When the butter sizzles, ladle in a scant 1/4 cup of the batter and tip the pan to coat the bottom and sides with a thin layer. Cook until the top of the crêpe is bubbly and the crêpe starts to come loose from the pan, about 30 seconds. Flip the crêpe over and cook until set, brown spots appear, and it slides easily from the pan. The crêpes should be light gold, thin, and cooked through. Cook the remaining batter in the same manner. As the crêpes are cooked, stack them.

To prepare the filling, in a bowl stir together the cottage cheese and bread crumbs.

To assemble the blintzes, place 3 tablespoons filling in the middle of each crêpe. Fold in the opposite sides to overlap a bit at the middle of the bundle. Then fold in the 2 remaining sides to form a "package." Turn the blintz over, fold side down.

Continue filling and folding until all the blintzes are made. At this point, they can be held in a refrigerator for up to 24 hours, or they can be kept frozen ≈

for up to 1 month. In either case, wrap tightly with plastic wrap.

To cook the blintzes, heat 1/4 cup of the butter in a large cast-iron skillet over medium heat until bubbly hot. Place 6 blintzes, seam sides down, in the skillet and cook until golden. Turn the blintzes and cook until quite brown and crispy. Allow the blintzes to remain in the pan long enough for the cheese to heat well and be mostly melted, 10 to 12 minutes. Cook the remainder of the blintzes in 2 more batches, using 1/4 cup butter for each batch.

Arrange 3 blintzes on each serving plate. Top each blintz with dollops of sour cream and jam.

Note: Most blintz recipes call for sugar in the filling or in the crêpe; this one does not and these blintzes are, I think, far better. The result is a sourdough French toast flavor. Also, you may be frustrated by the fact that you will have to discard the first 2 or 3 crêpes that come out of the pan, but this is to be expected. It usually takes a couple of throw-aways to "season" the pan and get the cooking temperature just right.

MEXICAN HOT CHOCOLATE

*U*sing Mexican chocolate makes this breakfast beverage so superior to the usual cocoa powder mixture that there is no comparison. Any self-respecting chocoholic should try this. It is rich and made more interesting with its cinnamon and almond flavors. Once you try this frothy chocolate drink, you'll probably never return to the powder. Mexican chocolate is available in large supermarkets, Latino markets, and from mail-order sources.

Serves 1

1 cup milk

1/2 tablet (1 ½ ounces) Ibarra or
    Abuelita brand Mexican chocolate,
    broken into 3 or 4 pieces

Heat the milk in a saucepan over medium heat until small bubbles begin to break on the surface.

Pour the heated milk into the jar of an electric blender. Add the chocolate and liquefy until frothy. Serve at once.

Note: If you have an espresso machine with a milk steamer-attachment, use it to make this hot chocolate. Grate the chocolate and place it in the bottom of the cup with the milk, then inject steam into the milk until it is frothy.

Windowsill at Cafe Pasqual's, facing Doodlet's Shop, Don Gaspar Street, Santa Fe, New Mexico.

CHORIZO SAUSAGE

*T*his Mexican sausage, made of pork, chile, spices, and herbs, may be made in links or in bulk. For the recipes in this book, however, only the bulk form is necessary. Chorizo freezes beautifully, so you may want to double or triple the recipe to have extra sausage on hand. Divide the freezer-destined sausage among small, plastic freezer bags. Small portions are easy to thaw, making them quickly available for use.

There are as many recipes for chorizo as there are cooks, so start with this list of ingredients and play with it, adding a little of this and a little of that. For instance, you may decide to use green chiles instead of red and then add jalapeño chile powder. *Arriba!* Test the results for taste and texture by cooking a tablespoon or so at a time in a medium-hot skillet. Be sure to dry roast the spices for added pungency and grind them in a coffee grinder or spice mill before using.

If you are using wonderfully fresh (that is, recently dried) *ancho* chiles, they may be quite leathery. Be sure to have a well-sharpened knife for the task of mincing the chiles. In lieu of a sharp knife, use kitchen scissors to cut the *anchos* into narrow strips and then cut those into small bits.

The *molido*, or chile powder, called for in the ingredients list is pure ground chile and is sold in cellophane packages at larger supermarkets or is available through mail order. Do not make this recipe with the chile powder commonly found on supermarket spice shelves. That product is too sweet and the sausage will not have the requisite zing.

Mexican cinnamon is delicate in flavor. The bark is softer than Batavian cinnamon, which is the variety most widely used. Batavian cinnamon is also much sharper in taste; it almost has a "sting" to its flavor. If possible, use the Mexican variety, available in Latino markets, large supermarkets, and through mail order. Look for *canela*, Spanish for "cinnamon," on the package.

Makes 1 pound

2 Mexican cinnamon sticks, each
    2 inches long

5 whole cloves

3/4 teaspoon cumin seeds

10 whole black peppercorns

1 tablespoon Chimayó chile powder

1 tablespoon medium-hot New Mexico
    chile powder (**molido**)

1/2 teaspoon kosher salt

4 large cloves garlic, finely minced

3 *ancho* chiles, stemmed, seeded, and
    finely chopped

1/4 cup red wine vinegar

1/4 cup water, or as needed

1 pound pork shoulder, coarsely
    ground (see note)

5 ounces pork fat, ground

Combine the cinnamon, cloves, cumin, and peppercorns in a small, dry nonstick sauté pan or cast-iron skillet over medium heat. Roast, shaking the pan frequently, until the aromas are released, about 2 minutes. Remove from the heat and let cool. Place the spices in a spice mill or coffee grinder to pulverize. Alternatively, pulverize in a mortar using a pestle.

Put all the ingredients, except the pork and pork fat, in a blender or in a food processor fitted with the metal blade. Run at high speed to form a paste. If more water is needed to achieve a paste, add it sparingly.

Place the ground pork and pork fat in a bowl and add the paste. Using a large spoon, combine the ingredients thoroughly. Cover and refrigerate for no more than 1 or 2 days. The chorizo may be frozen for up to 2 months.

Note: If possible, have your butcher grind the pork and pork fat. If you grind the pork at home, first freeze the meat and fat for about 2 hours so the fat will grind into discrete pieces. Use a food processor fitted with the metal blade and work quickly.

Cooking herbs and remedies, Lujan's Place, Santa Fe, New Mexico.

FIELD GREENS WITH FIRE-ROASTED POBLANO
CHILES IN BALSAMIC VINAIGRETTE

❖

HEARTS OF ROMAINE WITH MAYTAG BLUE,
TOASTED CHILE PECANS, AND SLICED PEAR

❖

A. J.'S ROMAINE AND SHRIMP SALAD
WITH GREEN GODDESS DRESSING

❖

WARM SALAD OF GRILLED PORTABELLO AND
SHIITAKE MUSHROOMS WITH LIVELY GREENS

❖

THAI BEEF AND MINT SALAD

❖

CHICKEN SALAD
WITH SESAME-MUSTARD DRESSING

SALADS

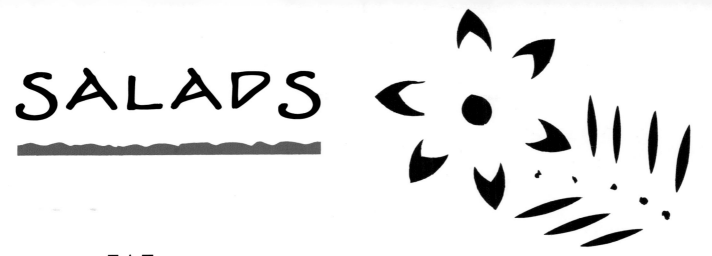

When local growers make their deliveries to our kitchen—and, incredibly, they all make the trip to town themselves to drop off the food personally—we inquire how their season is going, if cold weather is hindering the tomatoes, how the grasshoppers are out their way. We take the time with these colleagues, who are every bit as committed as we are to a fine product. Without them, we cannot so happily accomplish our art. Being part of the whole picture, understanding and knowing the source of the food, is an integrating experience, and one that inspires us to cook our very best at Cafe Pasqual's.

Occasionally, we pay our growers a visit. We had been buying red oakleaf lettuce from a brilliant, wizened farmer, Truman Brigham, for three years before we went to look over his place in the Española Valley, about thirty miles north of Santa Fe. Truman was delighted to tour us around the fifteen acres he has been tending for nearly fifty years. At the end of the visit, he walked us over to a vast landscape and pointed out six football-field-long rows of lettuce. "Over here is your red oakleaf lettuce," he said, smiling broadly and pointing with his arthritic finger. It was a sight all right. The lettuces looked like shiny bronze doilies set down on the hard, dry earth by some unseen child at play. And to some extent that is how they came to be in that field, because Truman takes genuine joy in growing and selling, and sharing, his lettuces.

It is more than "growers' charm" that makes me get in the truck and drive north for two and a half hours, then rattle down miles of rutted dirt roads, kicking into four-wheel drive at least twice, before finally arriving at Elizabeth and Fred Berry's Gallina Canyon Ranch, situated in the red-and-gray cliff canyon lands above Abiquiu. Only one other family in recorded history farmed the land before the Berrys—the family they bought it from. Before them it was home to the Anasazi, American Indian cliff dwellers who lived there from 600 to 1400.

After nearly an hour on the bumpy dirt trail to the Berry farm, I'm gratified to see the sloping roof of the all-pegs, no-nails elegant farmhouse with its outdoor summer kitchen. The Berrys run about a hundred head of cattle on their four hundred acres and farm four precious acres of it with a gravity spring-fed drip irrigation system of Fred's ingenious design—ingenious because the spring should only support one acre. Walking from the truck to the house by way of the cosmos flowers bobbing six feet high in the bright afternoon sun, I feel the transformation beginning. Beethoven is blaring from the house. The amplifier is turned as loud as it will go because the "plants love classical music," according to Elizabeth. Three men are tending the meticulous gardens in which I have never encountered a single weed. Under the guidance of Elizabeth and foreman José Duran, the most knowledgeable, determined grower this planet hosts, they stoop over the rows from dawn to dusk, making an Eden out of the dry high desert.

During their first summer of planting, Elizabeth and José encountered 127 rattlesnakes on the four acres. Now, some five summers later, they're happy to report just 38. Such statistics raise the question of why they farm there, so far from town, up such an unreliable, desolate route, with such a short season? Simple. It is a breathtakingly beautiful place. The Chama River winds along at the base of thousand-foot, multicolored sandstone canyon walls and the light plays an optical illusion with them all day, seeming alternately to bring them forward and push them back, dazzling one's perception.

Wonders abound in Elizabeth's garden. The leaves on the squash plants are nearly as large as the hood of a car. There are fifty tomato varieties, and as many chile varieties, thanks to Elizabeth's seed research every winter, calling around the country in search of heirloom strains. There are purple string beans from Japan and white eggplants as round as tennis balls. The magic in that canyon is palpable, and it is a humbling and awesome experience to go there.

It is not easy to be a grower in New Mexico. There are only about ninety growing days in the northern part of the state, where Santa Fe is located, and only ten inches of rain a year. Summer is the monsoon season, so when the rains fall—and that can be nearly daily for a month and then not a drop for the next—the downpours are fearsome with thunder and lightning, and often bring ankle-deep hail as big as a man's fist. Elizabeth keeps handy huge lengths of canvas to fling over the salad greens and herb plots at the first sight of a hailstorm.

Water—finding it and conserving it—is the number one political issue in desert places. More than six hundred years ago, the indigenous people began a network of irrigation systems to regulate and conserve the erratic water supply throughout the region. This same network is being used today. Known as the *acequia*, or "ditch system," these ditches are so revered and vital that one of Santa Fe's elementary schools is so-named for its location along the Acequia Madre, or "Mother Ditch."

Many of the growers I have been privileged to know in New Mexico are growers because they have no choice. Like artists anywhere, they are compelled to do their work, not because it is the easiest thing to do, or because it is the only thing to do, or because they inherited the land, but because they recognize a partnership and stewardship role with the earth deep within themselves. At Cafe Pasqual's we take their bounty and do our part to transform it into what we hope are memorable, nourishing dishes that retain the respect with which the raw ingredients were grown.

Salads can lure people into new ways to "get their greens," so at the restaurant we place a lot of importance on them. You can judge the quality of a kitchen by its salad offerings. If care and thought have gone into preparing these most perishable ingredients, the tender leaves and delicate shoots, then you can expect the same careful attention to the rest of the meal.

The following recipes are, quite simply, our patrons' favorites. They may be served as accompaniments or as main courses. We have offered our hearts of romaine salad at dinner as a generous plate meant to be shared. The warm grilled mushroom salad is a teaser—a light, great introduction to a dinner. The Thai-inspired beef and mint salad is a complete meal and quite unforgettable.

FIELD GREENS WITH FIRE-ROASTED POBLANO CHILES IN BALSAMIC VINAIGRETTE

*T*he stellar hot-sweet dressing that coats these garden-fresh greens was created by *chef extraordinaire* Sally Witham. It is Cafe Pasqual's house dressing and the recipe is often requested. *Poblano* chiles are becoming easier to find these days. They are rather wide and pointy, dark green, and mild (mostly). Alas, there is no substitute. If they are unavailable, cajole your grocer into special ordering these wonders for you. Balsamic vinegar is imported from Modena, Italy, where it is aged in wood for at least a dozen years. It is expensive, but worth its cost for its startlingly sweet, deep, delicious flavor. You will have about 3/4 cup vinaigrette. It is also good served over spinach leaves with crisp bacon pieces.

Serves 6

1/4 cup balsamic vinegar

1/3 cup plus 1 tablespoon soy oil or other vegetable oil

2 tablespoons olive oil

Scant 1/2 teaspoon ground cumin

Scant 1/2 teaspoon ground coriander

1/2 teaspoon kosher salt

About 1/4 pound fresh *poblano* chiles, roasted, peeled, seeded, and cut into 1/2-inch squares to measure 1/3 cup (page 22)

8 cups mixed seasonal field greens such as cress, oakleaf lettuce, red mustard, arugula, mizuna, dandelion, *tat soi*, and other fancy lettuces

In a small bowl stir together the vinegar, oils, cumin, coriander, and salt. Mix in the *poblanos*.

Place the field greens in a salad bowl and pour the dressing over the top. Toss to coat the leaves and serve.

Note: The dressing may be refrigerated for up to 1 week. Bring to room temperature before using.

Hearts of Romaine with Maytag Blue, Toasted Chile Pecans, and Sliced Pear

*S*cott Boac was our pantry cook at the time he invented this wildly popular salad. The addition of toasted chile pecans was a stroke of genius and our patrons agree—they order the pecans by the pound for parties and gifts! If you should have leftover dressing, it is terrific as a dip for raw vegetables. In fact it is habit-forming. Maytag blue cheese is a sharp, somewhat creamy blue cheese that is cave-ripened in Iowa! Your own favorite blue cheese may be substituted. For a variation, use Granny Smith apples instead of pears.

Serves 6 to 8 as a salad course, or 4 to 5 as a main course

4 heads romaine lettuce

For the Maytag blue dressing:

1/4 pound Maytag blue cheese (1/2 cup crumbled)

1/2 cup sour cream

1/2 cup buttermilk

1/4 cup half-and-half

2 ounces soft goat cheese (1/4 cup crumbled)

Juice from 1 orange

1 tablespoon minced, stemmed fresh mint leaves

2 teaspoons minced, stemmed fresh basil leaves

1/2 small shallot, minced

1/4 teaspoon salt

1/4 teaspoon cayenne pepper

Freshly ground black pepper

For the toasted chile pecans:

1 cup pecan halves

2 tablespoons vegetable oil

2 teaspoons Kahlúa liqueur

1 heaping tablespoon Chimayó chile powder

2 teaspoons granulated sugar

2 ripe but firm Bartlett pears, cored and sliced lengthwise

Freshly coarse-ground black pepper

3 or 4 lemons, halved and seeded

Use only the hearts of the romaine lettuces; reserve the outer leaves for another purpose. Separate, wash, and dry the lettuce leaves, then wrap in a cloth ≈

towel or paper towel and chill for at least 1 hour before serving. Keep the leaves whole, to be eaten with a fork and knife or with the fingertips.

To prepare the dressing, in a salad bowl combine all the ingredients, including black pepper to taste, and mix thoroughly with a wooden spoon. Taste and adjust the seasonings. Cover and refrigerate.

Preheat an oven to 300° F.

To prepare the pecans, in a bowl toss the nuts with the oil and Kahlúa liqueur until evenly coated. Then add the chile powder and sugar and toss again. Spread the nuts out on a baking sheet and place in the oven, stirring frequently, until toasted, about 25 minutes. Do not allow them to burn. Set aside to cool.

To assemble the salad, add the romaine leaves to the dressing and toss until every leaf is well coated. Place on individual plates and sprinkle the pecans over the leaves. Fan the pear slices out atop the romaine leaves. Grind black pepper over all, then squeeze half a lemon over each salad. Serve immediately.

A. J.'s Romaine and Shrimp Salad with Green Goddess Dressing

*T*his recipe comes from my Aunt June Shane. As a child, I was so enamored of this dressing that she would give me a mason jar of it as a gift at Christmas. It is tangy, salty, and sweet all at once, an engaging range of flavors, and better when served the day after it is made. Keep the dressing refrigerated until just before serving.

Serves 6 to 8

2 to 3 pounds large shrimp, peeled and deveined

3 to 4 heads romaine lettuce

For the green goddess dressing:

3/4 cup mayonnaise

1/2 cup fresh lemon juice, strained (about 4 lemons)

2 cups firmly packed, stemmed fresh parsley leaves

1 bunch scallions (about 6), including the green tops, coarsely chopped

1 can (2 ounces) anchovy fillets, drained

1 tablespoon granulated sugar

2 ripe avocados, peeled, pitted, and diced (optional)

Bring a saucepan filled with water to a boil. Add the shrimp and boil just until they turn pink, about 3 minutes. Drain, cover, and chill.

Use only the hearts of the romaine lettuces; reserve the large outer leaves for another purpose. Separate, wash, and dry the leaves, then wrap in a cloth towel or paper towel and chill for at least 1 hour before serving.

To prepare the dressing, combine all the ingredients in a blender and liquefy, 10 to 15 seconds.

To serve, tear the romaine leaves into 2-inch lengths and place in a salad bowl with the avocados, if using. Pour on the dressing and toss well to coat the leaves and avocados. Arrange the shrimp on top of the salad and serve.

WARM SALAD OF GRILLED PORTABELLO AND SHIITAKE MUSHROOMS WITH LIVELY GREENS

*H*ere is a must for those who adore the deep, mysterious flavors of the forest. The mushrooms and wood-aged balsamic vinegar are a perfect partnering. This is a simple recipe that achieves dazzling results. Portabello mushrooms are humongous and, once tasted, their earthy, woodsy, somewhat sweet flavor becomes the standard for heavenly fungi. They are becoming more readily available from the better markets, and are definitely worth a search or a special order from your grocer. If portabello mushrooms are unavailable, use all shiitakes or use other wild, flavorful mushrooms. This salad is wonderful served with thinly sliced French bread toast that has been brushed with a fruity olive oil or spread with goat cheese.

Serves 6 to 8 as a small salad, or 4 to 6 as a main course

4 cloves garlic, minced

2 tablespoons stemmed fresh thyme leaves

Juice of 1 lemon

2/3 cup balsamic vinegar

1 cup olive oil

6 fresh portabello mushrooms, stemmed and wiped clean with a dry towel

8 fresh shiitake mushrooms, stemmed and wiped clean with a dry towel

2 heads Belgian endive

1 small head radicchio

2 bunches arugula

Salt and freshly coarse-ground black pepper

In a shallow glass bowl, stir together the garlic, thyme, lemon juice, vinegar, and olive oil until well mixed. Add the mushrooms and marinate at room temperature for 1 to 2 hours.

Prepare a fire in a charcoal grill. Crisscross grill racks to form a meshed cooking surface, so the mushrooms do not fall through the grate. Alternatively, lay a piece of well-perforated aluminum foil across a portion of the grill rack to act as a guard.

Separate, wash, and dry the leaves of the Belgian endive, radicchio, and arugula. Set aside.

When the coals are ready, remove the mushrooms from the marinade. Pour the marinade into a saucepan over medium heat. Simmer for 2 minutes; do not allow it to boil. Keep the marinade warm.

Arrange the mushrooms on the grill rack or foil and grill the mushrooms, turning once, until heated through, 3 to 5 minutes on each side.

In a large salad bowl, combine the warmed marinade, mushrooms, and prepared leaves. Toss to coat well. Season to taste with salt and pepper. Serve immediately.

Elizabeth Berry, organic vegetable grower, at her Gallina Canyon Ranch, north of Abiquiu, New Mexico.

THAI BEEF AND MINT SALAD

Chef Laura Taylor invented this dish, which has become my favorite warm dinner salad. The flavors are utterly compelling. If there is any left over, it is wonderful cold for a midnight snack.

Serves 4 to 6

3/4 pound flank steak or beef loin flap

3 celery stalks

2 tablespoons Asian sesame oil, or as needed

2 tablespoons finely minced, peeled fresh ginger

5 cloves garlic, lightly crushed with the blade of a heavy knife or cleaver

1 tablespoon finely minced garlic

2 teaspoons minced fresh Thai chiles

5 Italian plum tomatoes or other firm, ripe tomatoes, cored and cut lengthwise into thin wedges

2 scallions, including the green tops, cut into 2-inch lengths

1/2 large red onion, thinly sliced lengthwise

Juice of 1 small lime

Few dashes of Thai fish sauce

2 cups stemmed fresh mint leaves

1/2 cup stemmed fresh cilantro (coriander) leaves

1 cup cut (2-inch squares) napa cabbage

1 package (4 to 6 ounces) bean-thread noodles, cooked and drained, or 4 cups hot steamed long-grain Basmati or Texmati rice (optional; see note)

To make the steak easier to slice, place it in a freezer for about 40 minutes. Cut the steak against the grain into very thin strips, and then crosswise into 2-inch lengths. Place each celery stalk on its side and cut at a 45-degree angle to achieve long, thin exaggerated V-shaped pieces.

Heat a wok or a very large cast-iron skillet over high heat. Add just enough oil to coat the pan, swirling it to coat the pan surfaces. Heat the oil until it is just smoking. Add the beef and sear it, stirring, until it browns. Add the ginger, garlic, and chiles and stir-fry for 1 minute. Add the celery, tomatoes, scallions, and red onions. Stir-fry until the celery just begins to soften, 3 to 5 minutes. Add the lime juice, fish sauce, and mint and cilantro leaves. If a juicier salad is desired, add a splash of water at this point. Remove from the heat.

Line a serving platter with the cabbage and spoon the salad over the top. Alternatively, to make a full-fledged main course, serve the salad over hot bean-thread noodles or steamed rice in addition to the cabbage.

Tina Le Marque-Earll and her daughter, Sasha, regulars at Pasqual's.

Note: Bean-thread noodles are available from gourmet grocers and Asian markets. To prepare, bring a saucepan filled with water to a boil, add the noodles, and boil until soft, about 5 minutes. Drain carefully! These noodles are so slippery they have a way of escaping from the strainer. Basmati is a type of rice grown in India. Texmati is a domestic rice similar to basmati, but less expensive. Both are available in large well-stocked supermarkets, gourmet outlets, and natural-food groceries.

CHICKEN SALAD WITH SESAME-MUSTARD DRESSING

*T*his acclaimed Chinese noodle salad played on our menu for ten years. A long run! Chinese cuisine has been a lifelong passion of mine. This salad was inspired by the cooking of my mentor-chef, Gabriel Chin. Gabriel lived in Ann Arbor in my "salad days" there, and he would invite over twenty or thirty friends to partake of his fabulous, joy-infused weekly banquets. The whole evening long he sang grand opera in his trained baritone voice as he wielded his cleaver and tossed a seemingly endless array of ingredients into his giant, old-fashioned cast-iron skillet. Gabriel didn't use a wok, believing woks weren't made for the American flat-top stove. Besides, he would point out, skillets got hotter than woks and distributed the heat more evenly. His feasts were often launched with this salad.

Serves 4

1 whole chicken breast, about 3/4
    pound, halved, boned, and skinned

6 to 8 ounces thin Chinese, Italian, or
    other egg noodles

3 cucumbers

2 eggs

2 teaspoons peanut oil

For the sesame-mustard dressing:

1/2 cup tahini (see note)

1/2 cup soy sauce

1/3 cup white wine vinegar

1 tablespoon Asian sesame oil

1 tablespoon dry mustard, or more
    to taste

1 tablespoon vegetable oil

1/4 pound cooked ham, cut into long,
    thin strips

Fresh cilantro (coriander) sprigs for
    garnish

Place the chicken breasts in a saucepan that is just large enough to accommodate them. Add water to cover and bring to a boil. Reduce the heat to low and simmer until the breasts are no longer pink on the inside, 10 to 15 minutes. Using a slotted spoon, remove the breasts from the water and let cool to room temperature, then shred by hand into long, thin pieces.

Fill a saucepan with water and bring to a boil. Add the noodles and boil until tender but still firm to the bite, just a few minutes. Drain and let cool. You should have about 4 cups. To prevent the cooling noodles from sticking together, place them in a container, add cold water to cover, and set aside. ≈

Hollowed log flume of acequia, or "ditch" system, Las Trampas. Located on the high road to Taos, New Mexico.

Cut the cucumbers in half lengthwise and scoop out the seeds with a teaspoon. Using the largest teeth on a hand grater, grate the cucumbers. Leave the peel on to protect your hand, then discard the peel. Squeeze the grated cucumber to extract any liquid and discard the liquid. Do not use a machine for this process, as the cucumbers will become mushy.

Break the eggs into a small bowl and beat vigorously with a fork 20 times. Heat a 7-inch non-stick pan over medium heat. When the pan is hot, add the peanut oil. When the oil is hot, add the eggs and cook until partially set, lifting the edges with a rubber spatula to let the uncooked egg flow underneath. Continue to cook the omelet until it is mostly set; there should be only a small pool of uncooked egg in the center. Turn the omelet by flipping it, or lifting it with a spatula. Cook for 3 minutes more. Remove from the heat and let cool to room temperature, then cut into long, thin strips.

To prepare the dressing, combine all the ingredients in a food processor fitted with the metal blade or in a blender and process until smooth. Taste and adjust with more mustard, if desired.

To assemble the salad, use individual plates or a large platter. Just before serving, put three fourths of the dressing in a bowl large enough to hold the noodles. Add the noodles and toss to coat well. Mound the noodles (volcanolike) in center of the plate(s). Put the shredded chicken in the "crater" on top, then place the ham and omelet strips in an alternating pattern radiating from the top of the mound. Top with the additional dressing and garnish with the cilantro sprigs.

Note: Tahini is sesame paste with the consistency of nut butter. It is found in natural-food groceries, Middle Eastern food stores, and gourmet markets.

MANGO-LEMON SOUP

❖

CHILLED AVOCADO AND GREEN CHILE SOUP

❖

MOM'S GREEN SPLIT PEA SOUP
WITH LAMB AND GARLIC SAUSAGE

❖

SOPA DE ALBONDIGAS

❖

CALDILLO DE FRIJOLES BLANCOS Y NEGROS

❖

CHICKEN-TOMATILLO SOUP

❖

TOM YUM

❖

CHICKEN STOCK

SOUPS

Down-home soup recipes must surely be the repositories of a family's collective memory. My mother's green split-pea soup with its rich lamb and garlic-flavored warmth always lulled the family into a timeless space of well-being. The preparation of her soup recipe took three days. It began with the incomparable aroma of a roasting leg of lamb.

On the first evening we dined on slices of the crusty, dark brown leg. The carving of the roast was so ritualized that I can see its choreography even now. My father stood at his place at the table with the plattered roast before him, filling the small dining nook with its heady aroma. He picked up the antler-handled carving knife and ceremoniously honed the blade with long strokes, taking his time to make sure the sharpest possible edge was achieved. This, of course, was excellent for the roast, as the juices could rest and be reabsorbed into the meat while our salivary glands began to work overtime.

Always accompanying the roast were potatoes, carrots, and yellow onion quarters, shiny wet with the dark juices. Each item was carefully and slowly served up to us by Dad amidst paeans of praise for Mom's cooking. Then a generous gravy boat was tilted and a dark brown river of thickened juices flowed over all. We luxuriated in each flavorful mouthful, smug in the knowledge that the best was yet to come.

As we went about the second evening's business of homework and newspaper reading, we kept an ear cocked to the sound of busy preparations in the kitchen. First, the caramelized garlic drippings were scraped from the roasting pan into the big stainless-steel pot. Also into the soup pot went the leftover roasted potatoes, carrots, onions, and gravy. Then in went the giant lamb bone, morsels of meat, a couple of pounds of dried green split peas, and, lastly, a good splash of water. The heavy pot was set to boil and yield up the gray, frothing foam that Mom would skim off and throw away.

At this point the perfume would begin. Slowly the soup cooked, filling the house and our senses with its gentle fragrance and memories of distant wet gardens. It was a long process, not arduous or anxious, just long, slow, sure, the part that makes soup a great experience: the patient waiting for the promise of nourishment to be fulfilled. It cooked for nearly two hours. The last sound from the kitchen that evening was the whirl of the blender. We slept contentedly that night knowing that no matter what hazard befell us the next day, all would be well when we gathered for Mom's soup.

The afternoon of the third day Mom would begin to reheat the soup very slowly. The biggest wooden spoon in the kitchen was employed to stir it every few minutes to bring it gradually to serving temperature. Fat garlic sausages were torn out of pink butcher paper, skinned, sliced into rounds, and put into the soup, with just enough time to heat through.

When at last the family sat down to the wondrously thick, garlicky, sausage-laden green split-pea soup, grateful praises were spoken almost in reverence, a reverence our family knew only at the table. We thanked Mom for taking the time to tend the family ritual that nourished and renewed us.

At Cafe Pasqual's soup is serious business. Our regular patrons depend upon us to satisfy their soup cravings. Every morning around 10:30 the phone starts jangling, and the question is, "What's the soup today?" The shopkeepers and downtown office dwellers expect, and get, ever-changing, salubrious, and flavorsome offerings.

MANGO-LEMON SOUP

A mango, to my taste, is the most sensuous of fruits, and I'm always looking for ways to celebrate it. This preparation is as simple as can be, and guaranteed to cool down the hottest summer day. Be sure to make it well in advance to allow for adequate chilling.

Serves 4

4 ripe mangoes

2 lemons

1 cup heavy cream

1 pint (2 cups) raspberries for garnish

Fresh mint sprigs for garnish

To pit the mangoes, rest each mango on a cutting board with the stem side up and narrow profile facing you. Using a large, sharp knife, cut straight down the mango 1 inch on either side of the stem. This will result in two pitless halves. (The pit is for the cook's enjoyment, to be gnawed on over the sink!) Peel the halves and chop coarsely.

Zest the lemons on a grater. Then juice them and strain out any seeds from the juice.

Put the mango and lemon juice in a food processor fitted with the metal blade or in a blender and liquefy. Pour off 2 cups of the purée for garnish; cover and refrigerate. Add the cream to the purée remaining in the processor or blender and pulse just to incorporate; do not leave the machine on for more than a few seconds or the mixture will be too thick because the cream whips up quickly. Transfer to a bowl and stir in three-fourths of the lemon zest and reserve the remainder for garnish. Cover and refrigerate to chill thoroughly before serving, at least 4 hours.

Ladle the chilled soup into individual bowls. Garnish each with a swirl of the reserved mango purée, some lemon zest and raspberries, and a mint sprig.

CHILLED AVOCADO AND GREEN CHILE SOUP

*T*his smoky, rich soup has truly unusual flavors. Use the curry powder sparingly. A discernible curry flavor should not be evident; it is included only to "spice up" the soup. Be cautious with the cayenne, too; its piquant quality can vary wildly from one source to another.

Serves 6 to 8

About 3/4 pound fresh green New Mexico chiles, roasted, peeled, seeded, and coarsely chopped to measure 1 cup (page 22)

6 ripe avocados, peeled, pitted, and coarsely cut

1/2 teaspoon curry powder

1/4 to 1/2 teaspoon cayenne pepper

2 to 4 cups milk

Salt

2 tablespoons finely minced red onion for garnish

Pauline Bustos, grower, Farmer's Market, Santa Fe, New Mexico

Combine the chiles, avocados, curry powder, cayenne pepper, and 2 cups of the milk in a blender. Whirl at high speed until all the ingredients are well incorporated and smooth. Add additional milk, if desired, for flavor and smoothness. Adjust to taste with salt. Cover and refrigerate to chill thoroughly before serving, at least 4 hours.

Ladle the chilled soup into individual bowls. Garnish each serving with the onion.

Mom's Green Split-Pea Soup with Lamb and Garlic Sausage

*I*nstead of the more traditional ham bone, this version of split-pea soup uses the bone from a roasted leg of lamb. Flavors will vary according to how many roast trimmings are left for the soup pot after a roast lamb dinner. This soup is leftover-dependent, so save up bits of roasted potato, carrot, garlic, onion, and gravy in the freezer until you have about six to eight cups. Most definitely a main course, this soup freezes beautifully, which may be a moot point since it gets better every day it is reheated. Serve with a simple salad and a good bread.

Serves 8 to 12

Bone from a roasted 6-pound or larger leg of lamb

4 to 5 cups (about 2 pounds) dried green split peas

2 to 4 cups cooked lamb morsels, trimmed from the lamb leg

4 to 6 cups gravy and coarsely chopped leftover oven-roasted potatoes, carrots, garlic, and onions

4 carrots, unpeeled, grated

6 quarts water, or as needed to cover

1 to 2 pounds garlic sausages or other cooked mild sausages, cut into 1/4-inch-thick slices

Salt and freshly coarse-ground black pepper

Put all the ingredients, except the sausages, salt, and pepper, into an 8-quart soup pot and bring to a gentle boil over medium-high heat. Skim off any foam that forms on the surface and discard. Reduce the heat to low and simmer, uncovered, until the split peas have begun to break down and are soft, 1 1/2 to 2 hours. The water will simmer away and the peas will expand, so be sure to stir frequently, scraping the bottom of the pot to keep the soup from scorching. Add water as needed to keep all the ingredients covered. When the peas are cooked, remove the bone.

Working in batches, purée the soup in a blender or in a food processor fitted with the metal blade until smooth. Return the soup to the pot over low heat and add the sausage slices. Heat gently until the soup and sausages are heated through. Add salt and pepper to taste. It is imperative to use freshly ground black pepper in this recipe! Serve very hot.

Note: When reheating the soup, add water during the warming process as needed to achieve a good consistency, keeping the soup fairly thick. Be careful reheating this soup as it can scorch easily. Stir frequently over very low heat. You may want to reheat it in a double boiler to avoid scorching.

SOPA DE ALBÓNDIGAS

*T*his light meatball soup is a personal favorite of mine. Not only do I love the flavors and texture, but I love to say *albóndigas!* Chef Gabriel Ruiz brought this recipe north from his family's ranch in Durango, Mexico, and for years this was the "Saturday soup" at Cafe Pasqual's. For a variation, prepare the meatballs using ground lean lamb instead of beef. Mint can stand in for the cilantro but use only half as much mint.

Serves 8

4 quarts Chicken Stock (page 87)

2 pounds ground lean beef

2 teaspoons ground cumin

**1 bunch fresh cilantro (coriander),
    stemmed and roughly chopped**

1/2 large white onion, finely chopped

2 tablespoons all-purpose flour

1 teaspoon salt

**Fresh cilantro sprigs for garnish
    (optional)**

Put the chicken stock into a large pot and bring slowly to a boil.

Meanwhile, combine the beef, cumin, chopped cilantro, onion, flour, and salt in a large bowl. Mix together well. Form into walnut-sized balls.

Gently slip the meatballs into the boiling stock, reduce the heat to low, and simmer until cooked through, about 25 minutes. Cut a meatball open to test for doneness before serving.

Ladle into individual bowls and serve garnished with cilantro sprigs, if desired.

Caldillo de Frijoles Blancos y Negros

Chef Martin Wright created this fabulous soup of white and black beans. Its hot, sweet, and somewhat salty character makes it a perfect cold weather dish—a hearty soup that is not for the timid. You can soften the flavors by reducing the amount of chiles and brandy, but you may find yourself putting the piquant peppers and liquor right back in!

Serves 6 to 8

2 cups (about 1 pound) dried small
    white beans such as Great Northern
    or navy

2½ quarts water, or as needed to cover

1/2 pound thick-sliced bacon, finely
    diced (see note)

7 fresh *serrano* chiles, stemmed and
    finely minced

1/2 small white onion, finely minced

1 cup brandy

Salt and freshly coarse-ground black
    pepper

1 cup Black Beans (page 38)

Finely chopped fresh parsley or cilantro
    (coriander) for garnish

Place the white beans and the water in a large pot. Bring to a boil, reduce the heat to low, and simmer, tightly covered, until the beans are tender but the skins have not split, 1½ to 2 hours. Add boiling water as needed to keep the water level constant and the beans just covered with liquid at all times.

Place the bacon in a skillet over medium-high heat and fry until crisp. Remove the bacon using a slotted utensil; reserve the bacon fat in the pan. Add the *serrano* chiles and onion to the skillet and sauté over medium heat until the onion is translucent, 5 to 10 minutes. Add the brandy and raise the heat. Deglaze the pan by scraping the bottom to dislodge any browned bits and boiling the mixture for 2 minutes. Empty the contents of the skillet into the beans and stir well. Add salt and pepper to taste.

Meanwhile, place the black beans in a saucepan over medium-low heat and heat to serving temperature, stirring frequently to prevent scorching.

To serve, ladle the white beans into individual bowls. Top each serving with about 2 tablespoons of the black beans. Garnish with parsley or cilantro.

CHICKEN-TOMATILLO SOUP

A soul-satisfying soup that is easy to expand for a crowd. For a delicious and aesthetic touch, serve the soup with charcoal-grilled (or boiled) corn on the cob in lieu of the kernels. Cut the cooked cobs into thirds and float them in the individual servings. Do not stint on the fresh cilantro; it is essential for a tantalizing result. Flat-leaf parsley may be substituted for those who dislike cilantro.

Serves 6 to 8

1 ½ tablespoons olive oil

1/2 red onion, finely minced

6 cloves garlic, finely minced

2 celery stalks, including leaves, cut into 1/4-inch slices

3 dried red New Mexico chiles, rinsed, stemmed, seeded, and chopped into small pieces

2 teaspoons ground cumin

1 tablespoon paprika

8 cups Chicken Stock (page 87)

20 tomatillos, husks removed, cut into quarters

5 tablespoons (3 ounces) tomato paste

2 cups fresh or frozen corn kernels

2 teaspoons granulated sugar

About 3/4 pound fresh mild green chiles, roasted, stemmed, peeled, seeded, and cut into long, thin strips to measure 1 cup (page 22)

1 whole chicken breast, about 3/4 pound

Salt and freshly coarse-ground black pepper

1/2 cup fresh cilantro (coriander) leaves, stemmed and finely minced, for garnish

In a large soup pot, heat the olive oil until quite hot. Add the onion, garlic, celery, and dried chiles and sauté for 5 minutes. Stir in the cumin and paprika. When the spices are incorporated, add the stock, tomatillos, tomato paste, corn, sugar, and green chiles. Add the chicken breast and simmer until the breast is cooked through, 15 to 20 minutes.

Using a slotted utensil, remove the breast from the stock. Continue to simmer the stock while the breast cools until it can be handled. Bone and skin the cooled breast, then shred the meat. Add the shredded chicken to the soup pot to heat through, about 3 minutes. Season to taste with salt and pepper.

Ladle the soup into individual bowls and garnish with the cilantro just at the moment of serving.

TOM YUM

*H*ere is the national soup of Thailand. It is so versatile you may use fish, shellfish, pork, beef, or chicken as the central ingredient, or keep it vegetarian with the addition of greens. A note following the recipe discusses the more exotic ingredients that go into it. Laura Taylor, Cafe Pasqual's chef for many years, took a sabbatical in Thailand and brought back this excellent recipe.

Serves 6 to 8

1½ pounds fish fillet, boned chicken breast meat, pork loin, or flank steak, or shellfish such as scallops, shrimp, or mussels in the shell

2 teaspoons Asian sesame oil

4 large cloves garlic

1 tablespoon peanut oil

1-inch piece fresh ginger, cut on the diagonal into slices 1/4 inch thick

4 or 5 fresh Thai chiles

5 kaffir lime leaves

1½ stalks lemongrass, cut on the diagonal into 1-inch lengths (see note)

2 large celery stalks, cut on the diagonal into long, thin slices

Celery leaves from 1 bunch celery, roughly chopped

1/2 red onion, sliced in thin, lengthwise strips

2 tablespoons Chimayó chile powder or any mild chile powder

4 Italian plum tomatoes, cored and cut lengthwise into thin wedges

8 cups water

1 tablespoon Thai fish sauce, or more to taste

2 cups stemmed fresh cilantro (coriander) leaves

1 lime, cut into quarters, for serving

Fresh cilantro sprigs for serving

If using fish fillets or chicken, cut into 1-inch cubes. If using pork or flank steak, thinly slice and then cut into long strips. If using shellfish, clean the scallops of their muscle, peel and devein the shrimp, or scrub the beard from the mussels.

Put 1 teaspoon of the sesame oil in a small cast-iron skillet over high heat. Add the garlic cloves and sauté until softened and lightly browned, about 5 minutes. Remove from the heat and reserve.

Put the peanut oil and the remaining 1 teaspoon sesame oil in a large stockpot over medium-high heat. When the oils are hot, add the ginger, chiles, lime leaves, lemongrass, celery, celery leaves, onion, ≈

chile powder, and sautéed garlic. Sauté, stirring occasionally, until the onion softens, 5 to 10 minutes.

Add the prepared seafood or meat and the tomatoes. Sear the meat or fish well on all sides for 5 minutes. Add the water and bring to a boil. Add the fish sauce and cilantro leaves, reduce the heat to low, and simmer for 30 minutes. Taste and adjust the seasonings. Add additional fish sauce judiciously if the soup is not salty enough.

Ladle into individual bowls. Serve with lime wedges and cilantro sprigs for each diner to add as desired.

Note: The condition of lemongrass stalks varies widely from source to source, so use only the tender portions. You may need to peel off and discard the dried outer leaves. Use the entire stalk, discarding only the top one-fourth of the leaves and the bottom inch of the root end. You may freeze Thai chiles and lemongrass so you have them on hand. (The limited availability of lemongrass forces the Cafe Pasqual's staff to freeze it on occasion; unfortunately, some flavor and texture are lost in the process.)

Do not attempt to eat the lemongrass, ginger pieces, or chiles in the finished soup; they're in the soup only for the the flavors they impart. You may want to remove them before serving. Be very, very cautious about eating the Thai chiles. They are not for the fainthearted and can sometimes be quite brutal when ingested.

Fish sauce varies, so ask the grocer for the least salty brand. The lime leaves, fish sauce, lemongrass, and sesame oil are available from Asian grocers. Thai chiles are more widely available; check for them in the produce sections of well-stocked supermarkets.

CHICKEN STOCK

A rich, concentrated chicken stock is a necessity for preparing full-flavored soups, sauces, and main dishes. Made ahead and kept frozen in convenient quantities, chicken stock is a true luxury for the cook and well worth the relatively small extra effort. If you do end up using commercially prepared chicken stock, be sure the can is labeled "reduced salt." It will be far better than the more widely available saltier product.

Makes about 4 quarts

4 to 5 pounds chicken backs

6 carrots, peeled

1 bunch fresh parsley, including stems

2 large yellow onions, quartered

5 to 6 quarts cold water

Combine all the ingredients in a stockpot. Bring to a boil over high heat.

Skim off any foam that forms on the surface and turn down the heat so that the stock is at a rolling simmer. Simmer, uncovered, for 2½ to 3 hours; the longer you simmer the stock, the richer the flavor will be.

Line a strainer with cheesecloth and place it over a large bowl or other container. Pour in the stock. Let cool and then store in a tightly covered container in the refrigerator for up to 2 days.

Before using the stock, remove the fat that has solidified on its surface. Reserve the fat for another use or discard. Bring the stock to a boil and boil for 5 minutes; this step rids it of any bacteria that may have formed in it. The stock can now be used in another recipe, or it may be cooled and frozen for up to 2 months. Store some of it by first freezing it in ice-cube trays and then removing the cubes to a plastic bag. This makes the stock easy to use as needed in small quantities.

Grilled Salmon Burrito with Goat Cheese
and Cucumber Salsa

❖

Grilled Free-Range Chicken Breast Sandwich
with Caramelized Onions and Jalapeños
and Manchego Cheese on Chile Corn Bread

❖

Carne Asada
with Guacamole and Salsa Fresca

❖

Chicharrónes Burritos

❖

Oaxacan Tamales

❖

Pablo's Cilantro-Pesto Quesadillas

LUNCH

At lunchtime the activity in the cafe's dining room really heats up. Customers pour in, locals and visitors alike. The room is abuzz with friends greeting each other, take-out orders being picked up, and waitpeople delivering platters of food and bowls of soup.

Pasqual's small dining room, some nine hundred square feet, is a simple rectangle. There is a platform seating area by a large window—an ideal perch from which to watch the streetlife or the noontime bustle in the room. In the center of the main level is the community table. When I started the cafe, I brought in my own dining room table, an antique oak table that I had purchased during my student days in Ann Arbor, Michigan. Little did I know then that one day all three leaves would be in place, that it would stand in my own eating establishment, and that it would host hundreds of thousands of meals.

The community table concept is a unique and favorite feature of the cafe. Its ten chairs seat solo diners or large parties. Being oval, it encourages interaction, although one may just as easily read, or write, or people watch. Potluck determines with whom you'll be sitting. We know of two babies who were named Pasqual because their parents met at the community table! A construction worker, an artist, an architect, and a visitor from New York may find themselves temporary companions. I love the democratic aspect of that old oak table. Regular breakfast customers fairly sink the table with newspapers, while the lunch patrons seem to converse more. Connections are made, information exchanged, stories told.

In this chapter you will find hearty fare, interpretations of both Old and New Mexican cuisine. The salmon-filled burrito is a new twist on the traditional tortilla-wrapped package, while the burrito, stuffed with *chicarrónes* and refried beans, is a northern New Mexican lunch staple.

Our quesadillas may be the perfect toasted cheese sandwich, with a tortilla cooked to a turn and salsa served on the side for zip. The Oaxacan tamales make a perfect light lunch with a cold Mexican beer.

GRILLED SALMON BURRITO WITH GOAT CHEESE AND CUCUMBER SALSA

Now and then a staff member walks up and hands me a gold nugget. Chef Sally Witham did just that the day she gave me this brilliant adaptation of the burrito that includes salmon, goat cheese, and, yes, black beans, all in a perfect combination that has enjoyed ovations since the day it went on the menu. The acidity of the lively, crunchy cucumber salsa is a light counterbalance to the richness of the salmon, cheese, and beans.

Serves 4

For the cucumber salsa:

2 cucumbers, peeled, seeded, and cut
    crosswise into 1/4-inch-thick slices

1/4 red onion, finely diced

1/2 red bell pepper, seeded, deveined,
    and finely diced

1/2 yellow bell pepper, seeded,
    deveined, and finely diced

1/4 bunch fresh cilantro (coriander),
    stemmed and coarsely chopped

1 teaspoon fresh dill leaves, finely
    chopped

1 fresh *serrano* chile, stemmed, seeded,
    and finely minced

2 teaspoons olive oil

3 teaspoons red wine vinegar

2 or 3 pinches of salt

For the salmon burrito:

2 teaspoons finely minced, stemmed
    fresh thyme leaves

2 teaspoons finely minced, stemmed
    fresh basil leaves

2 teaspoons finely minced, stemmed
    fresh Italian flat-leaf parsley

1/2 cup (about 1/4 pound) creamy goat
    cheese

4 salmon fillets, 6 ounces each

2 tablespoons Chimayó chile powder

1/4 cup olive oil

3 cups Black Beans (page 38)

4 large flour tortillas

To prepare the salsa, in a large bowl gently toss together all the ingredients until thoroughly mixed. This salsa may be prepared up to 1 hour before serving.

To prepare the burrito, combine the thyme, basil, parsley, and goat cheese in a small mixing bowl. Using a rubber spatula, fold and stir together until well mixed. Cover and refrigerate until ready to assemble the burrito.
≈

Prepare a fire in a charcoal grill. Check the salmon fillets carefully for pinbones by running your fingertips along the flesh side of the fillet. Remove any bones with pliers or tweezers. In a small bowl stir together the chile powder and olive oil. Rub each fillet on all sides with the oil mixture.

When the coals are hot, place the salmon fillets on the grill rack about 6 inches above the coals and grill, turning once, 2 to 3 minutes on each side, depending upon preferred degree of doneness and thickness of the fillets.

While the fillets are cooking, put the beans in a saucepan over medium-low heat and heat to serving temperature, stirring frequently to prevent scorching.

Warm the tortillas by placing them, one at a time, in a dry cast-iron skillet over high heat. Turning them once, heat for about 15 seconds on each side. Do not heat them too long or they will lose their pliability. Keep the tortillas warm by wrapping them in a dry cloth towel.

To assemble each burrito, place a tortilla on a warmed serving plate. Using a rubber spatula, spread 2 tablespoons of the seasoned goat cheese onto the tortilla. Place one-fourth cup of the beans in the center of each tortilla and top with a salmon fillet. Roll up the tortilla and place on a serving plate, fold side down. Top each burrito with the salsa, dividing it evenly among the servings. Serve immediately.

GRILLED FREE-RANGE CHICKEN BREAST SANDWICH WITH CARAMELIZED ONIONS AND JALAPEÑOS AND MANCHEGO CHEESE ON CHILE CORN BREAD

*E*ven though this succulent sandwich requires a lot of preparation, the recipe is often requested. It was a fun sandwich to create. Chef Sally Witham and I pitched the different components back and forth to each other. I said, "Let's do a grilled chicken sandwich." She responded, "Let's use caramelized onions and jalapeños." I said, "Let's put it on corn bread with *manchego.*" It took only seconds to create, but considerably longer to develop. We hope you will enjoy our offering. A palette of fresh fruit is a good accompaniment. Use any leftover corn bread to make great tasting toast.

Free-range chicken is raised without antibiotics. Unlike most commercial chickens, free-range chickens are not tied to perches or kept crammed for a lifetime in chicken houses. They roam, eat only grains, and lead a natural barnyard life. As a result, the meat is moist, tender, and far superior in flavor to that of their commercial cousins. Free-range chickens are also more expensive, but we demand superior products and are proud to serve our customers the best. Once you try a free-range chicken, I doubt you will turn to the commercial shelves again. (Free-range chickens have a much stronger aroma than commercial-grade chickens. As with all chickens, rinse and pat dry as a first step in preparation.)

Serves 6

For the chicken:

6 chicken breast halves, preferably free-range, boned

1/2 cup olive oil

3 tablespoons finely chopped garlic

For the chile corn bread:

1/2 cup warm water (110° F)

2 tablespoons yeast

1/2 cup vegetable oil

1/2 cup fresh or thawed frozen corn kernels, well drained

4 eggs

1 tablespoon salt

1 tablespoon sugar

1 tablespoon red pepper flakes

About 1/2 pound fresh green New Mexico, or Anaheim, or *poblano* chiles, roasted, peeled, seeded, and chopped to measure 3/4 cup (page 22)

Pinch of Chimayó chile powder

1 teaspoon baking soda

1 1/2 cups heavy cream

1 cup yellow cornmeal

8 1/2 cups all-purpose flour

Solid vegetable shortening or nonstick
    spray coating for loaf pans

For the caramelized onions and jalapeños:

3 tablespoons olive oil

3 yellow onions, sliced lengthwise into
    2-inch lengths

6 fresh jalapeño chiles, stemmed and
    cut crosswise into 1/8-inch-thick
    slices

1/3 cup granulated sugar

3/4 cup mayonnaise or *Serrano
    Mayonnaise* (pages 133–34)

1 1/2 cups grated *manchego* cheese

To prepare the chicken, place the breasts in a large, shallow glass bowl. Add the olive oil and garlic and turn the breasts to coat well. Cover and refrigerate for at least 4 hours, or for up to 48 hours.

To prepare the corn bread, combine the water, yeast, vegetable oil, and corn in a large bowl and stir together using a wooden spoon. Let stand until foamy, 10 to 12 minutes. Add all the remaining ingredients and mix well until the ingredients come together to form a dough. Turn out onto a lightly floured board and knead until smooth, about 10 minutes.

Form the dough into a ball and place in a large oiled bowl. Cover the bowl with a cloth towel and let the dough rise in a warm place until doubled in size, 45 minutes to 1 hour.

Grease two 5-by-9-inch loaf pans with either solid vegetable shortening or nonstick vegetable spray. Punch down the dough and divide it in half. Shape each half into a loaf and place in the prepared pans. Cover with a towel and let rise again until doubled in size, 30 to 45 minutes. Meanwhile, preheat an oven to 350° F.

Place the loaves in the oven and bake until they sound hollow when tapped on the top, about 1 hour. Remove the loaves from the oven, turn out of the pans immediately onto racks, and let cool completely.

To caramelize the onions and chiles, warm the oil in a 10-inch sauté pan over medium-high heat. Add the onions and sauté, stirring frequently, until translucent, about 20 minutes. Add the jalapeños and sugar and sauté until the jalapeños are soft and the onions are golden, 5 to 7 minutes. Remove from the heat and set aside.

Prepare a fire in a charcoal grill. Remove the chicken breasts from the marinade and place on the grill rack about 6 inches above medium-hot coals. Grill, turning once, until cooked, 4 to 6 minutes per side depending upon their thickness.

To assemble the sandwiches, preheat a broiler and select 6 flameproof serving plates or use a baking sheet. Cut twelve 1-inch-thick slices of corn bread. Spread the slices on one side with the mayonnaise. Divide the onions and chiles evenly among 6 of the slices. Top each with a grilled chicken breast. Pat 1/4 cup of the *manchego* cheese on top of each chicken breast. Run the plates or baking sheet under the broiler until the cheese melts, about 4 minutes.

Top each sandwich with a second slice of bread, mayonnaise side down, and cut in half on the diagonal. Serve immediately.

Carne Asada with Guacamole and Salsa Fresca

*C*arne *asada* means "broiled meat" in Spanish. Chef Martin Anton originated this "hot" version of the classic grilled beef dish. This is spectacular cuisine! It is delicious served with guacamole, salsa, and warm tortillas. Be sure to offer Mexican beer; my favorites are Bohemia for a light brew and Negra Modelo if you want dark beer. If you cannot locate jalapeño chile powder in your local market, it can be ordered through the mail.

The meat used for *asada* is beef loin flap, commonly referred to as *fajita* meat. The loin flap is the cut running along the ribs. This is an inexpensive cut but sometimes difficult to obtain. By all means search it out; it makes the juiciest, most flavorful *asada*. Many butchers sell skirt steak for use in making *fajitas*. This steak resembles the loin flap but is actually cut from the diaphragm. You may substitute skirt or flank steak but the results will not be as dazzling. A small portion of *Posole* Stew (page 43) makes an ideal side dish.

Serves 6 to 8

1 ¼ cups olive oil

2 tablespoons plus 2 teaspoons
  jalapeño chile powder

2 tablespoons Chimayó chile powder

3 tablespoons chopped garlic

1 tablespoon kosher salt

2 teaspoons red pepper flakes

1 teaspoon freshly ground black
  pepper

2 tablespoons fresh lime juice

3 red onions, cut into quarters and
  separated into pieces

3 pounds beef loin flap, very thinly
  sliced with the grain, cut into
  3- to 5-inch-long pieces

6 to 12 white-flour or whole-wheat
  tortillas

3 cups Guacamole (page 42)

3 cups *Salsa Fresca* (page 41)

In a large glass bowl, stir together the olive oil, jalapeño and Chimayó chile powders, garlic, salt, red pepper flakes, black pepper, lime juice, and onions. Put the steak slices in this mixture and turn them several times to coat well with the marinade. Cover and marinate in the refrigerator for up to 24 hours.

Prepare a fire in a charcoal grill. Crisscross grill grates to form a meshed cooking surface, so the grilling foods do not fall through the grate. Alternatively, lay a piece of well-perforated aluminum foil across a portion of the grill to act as a guard.

Preheat an oven to 250° F. In a dry cast-iron skillet over high heat, heat the tortillas one at a time, turning once, about 15 seconds on each side. Do not heat them too long or they will lose their pliability. Keep the tortillas warm by wrapping them in a dry cloth towel and placing in the oven.

Remove the meat strips from the marinade and place the meat and onion pieces on the grill rack about 6 inches above the medium-hot coals. Grill the meat and onions for 1 to 2 minutes on each side, working quickly to retain the moisture of the beef.

To serve, place a few tablespoons of guacamole on each serving plate along with a helping of the meat and onions, and a warmed tortilla. Have the salsa in a bowl on the table. Guests may eat the components separately or wrap them in a tortilla to make a burrito to eat out of hand.

Roadside produce stand, back room, stringing chile ristras during harvest, Hatch, New Mexico.

CHICHARRÓNES BURRITOS

*T*his recipe comes from the gracious Léona Tiede of Léona's de Chimayó. Léona's cooking is legendary in northern New Mexico. She has been preparing the very best regional fare and selling it from her open-air stand near the church in Chimayó for many years. This is her recipe for *chicharrónes*, which are crispy bits of pork fat with meat. *Chicharrónes* stirred into a pan of refried pintos, wrapped in a flour tortilla, and topped with green chile sauce make a hearty, savory lunch. To order Léona's delicious whole-wheat tortillas, see Mail-Order Sources on page 154. If you cannot wait to make the burritos, use white-flour tortillas.

Serves 4

1 pound fresh pork fat with meat attached but without the rind, cut into 1-inch squares (see note)

1/4 cup water

Salt

3 cups Refried Pinto Beans (page 40)

2 cups Green Chile Sauce (pages 34–35)

4 large whole-wheat tortillas

In a large skillet over medium heat, fry the pork pieces in the water until crispy and golden brown, 20 to 30 minutes. Remove to paper towels to drain. Sprinkle with salt to taste.

Heat the refried beans in a large skillet over low heat, stirring frequently. Stir the *chicharrónes* into the hot refried beans.

Place the chile sauce in a saucepan over medium-low heat and heat to serving temperature, stirring frequently to prevent scorching.

In a dry cast-iron skillet over high heat, heat the tortillas one at a time, turning once, about 15 seconds on each side. Do not heat them too long or they will lose their pliability. Keep the tortillas warm by wrapping them in a dry cloth towel.

To assemble the burritos, distribute an equal amount of the beans and chile sauce evenly down the middle of each tortilla. Roll up the tortilla and serve at once.

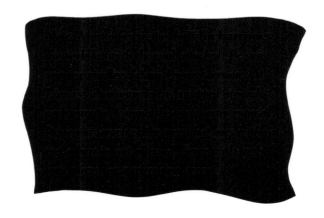

OAXACAN TAMALES

I first had these tamales some twenty years ago in a sidewalk cafe on the *zocálo* in Oaxaca. The earthy sweetness of the *tamal* wrapped in banana leaves has stayed with me as the most satisfying harmony of flavors of any meal I've ever had. The following recipe is an interpretation of that simple black bean *tamal*. At the cafe we've added a dollop of *mole*, and some Monterey Jack cheese, corn, and green chile. If you can find dried avocado leaves at a Latino market, buy a package. Tuck one leaf into each *tamal* for an added ethereal sweetness. You may want to play with the black beans, too; try them refried with fresh chiles or red pepper flakes.

Since the banana plant is native to the tropical highlands of Mexico near Oaxaca, banana leaves, rather than corn husks, are the wrap for this *tamal*. The leaves are available at any good Asian market. They are well worth using, as the distinctive flavor they impart to these tamales has been known to cause severe, yet exquisite reverie!

Makes 12 tamales; serves 6

1 package (about 1 pound) frozen
    banana leaves, thawed

3 cups *Masa* (page 45)

2 cups *Mole* (pages 128–29)

1 cup Black Beans (page 38)

1½ cups grated Monterey Jack cheese

About 3/4 pound fresh New Mexico
    green chiles, roasted, peeled,
    seeded, and chopped to measure
    1 cup (page 22)

1 cup fresh or thawed, frozen corn
    kernels, well drained

12 dried avocado leaves (optional)

Using scissors or the tip of a sharp knife, cut the banana leaves into 12 rectangles each measuring 6 by 8 inches. Make 24 ties for the tamales by ripping off 1/4-inch-wide strips the length of a leaf.

To assemble each *tamal*, place 1/4 cup *masa* in the center of a banana leaf rectangle and, using the heel of your hand and your fingertips, spread it 1/8 inch thick, leaving a 1-inch border of leaf uncovered. If you prefer, use a wet rubber spatula to spread the *masa*. Spoon about 2½ tablespoons of the *mole* onto the *masa*, then mound 4 teaspoons of the black beans in the center of the *mole*.

Place 2 tablespoons of the cheese on top of the beans and top with 4 teaspoons each of the green chiles and the corn. As the final step in assembling the *tamal*, lay an avocado leaf, if using them, on top of the layered ingredients.

To wrap the *tamal*, fold in the two longer sides of the banana leaf to overlap the midpoint of the mounded ingredients. Flatten the *tamal* a little by gently pressing down on the top with the palm of your hand. Now fold in the end flaps to make a package measuring 6 by 3 inches. Tie up each *tamal*   ≈

as you would a parcel, using 2 banana leaf strips as the tie for each package.

In a steamer large enough to accommodate all the tamales in a single layer (or use 2 steamers), arrange the tamales on a rack over gently boiling water. Cover and steam for 1 hour. Check the water frequently and add more water as needed to maintain the original level.

Serve immediately, setting out 2 tamales per person.

Note: Oaxacan tamales are not served with salsa or chile sauce. They are often simply accompanied by a cold Mexican beer. A stacking steamer (aluminum or bamboo), found in Asian hardware or cooking stores, is a worthwhile investment. With this type of steamer you have the option of steaming just a few tamales, or you can add layers of steamer racks or baskets and steam enough tamales to feed a crowd.

PABLO'S CILANTRO PESTO QUESADILLAS

Cook Paul Hudack contributed this recipe. It is rich and makes a great New Mexican toasted cheese sandwich. You may want to add some prosciutto and garnish the plate with melon, or serve a green salad alongside. There is plenty of room for innovation here, so dream up your own toasted-cheese-in-tortilla creation.

Makes 4 quesadillas; serves 2 as a large lunch or 4 as a light meal

1/2 cup olive oil

Juice of 2 limes

1 tablespoon fresh marjoram leaves, stemmed and finely minced

1 ½ pounds chicken breasts, preferably free-range, boned, skinned, and cut into long 1-inch-wide strips

For the cilantro pesto:

1 cup loosely packed fresh cilantro (coriander) leaves

2 cloves garlic

2 tablespoons piñon nuts, lightly toasted

2 tablespoons olive oil

2 tablespoons fresh lemon juice

2 tablespoons freshly grated Parmesan cheese

Salt and freshly ground black pepper

1/4 cup unsalted butter

4 white-flour or whole-wheat tortillas

3/4 cup grated Monterey Jack cheese

Salsa Fresca **(page 41)**

In a glass bowl, stir together the olive oil, lime juice, and marjoram. Add the chicken strips and toss to coat evenly. Cover and marinate in the refrigerator for at least 4 hours or for up to 24 hours.

To prepare the pesto, put all of the ingredients in a blender or in a food processor fitted with the metal blade and process until smooth. You may prepare this pesto up to 2 hours before serving, but do not expect it to keep overnight, as cilantro is fragile and its color changes and flavor fades within hours.

Prepare a fire in a charcoal grill. Crisscross grill racks to form a meshed cooking surface, to prevent the chicken strips from falling through the grate. Alternatively, lay a piece of well-perforated aluminum foil across a portion of the grill to act as a guard.

Preheat an oven to 250° F. ≈

Remove the chicken from the marinade and place on the grill rack about 6 inches above medium-hot coals. Grill quickly, turning once, until done, 1 to 3 minutes on each side. Remove to a dish and cover to keep warm.

To cook the quesadillas, put the butter in a cast-iron skillet over medium-high heat. When the butter sizzles, put in 1 tortilla, let it crisp on one side, about 2 minutes, and then turn it over. Spoon 2 tablespoons of the pesto, 3 tablespoons of the cheese, and one-fourth of the chicken onto one-half of the tortilla, then fold over the other half to cover the filling. Continue cooking the quesadilla until crisp and the cheese melts, about 5 more minutes. Remove the quesadilla to the warm oven to hold while you cook the others.

Serve the quesadillas piping hot with salsa on the side.

Chile ristras *and corn, Velarde, New Mexico.*

Whole Roasted Garlic with Asadero or Brie
Cheese and Tomatillo-Cilantro Salsa

❖

Corn Cakes with Calabacitas
and Queso Blanco Salsa

❖

Oaxacan Mangoes

❖

Steamed Mussels with Thai Basil
and Lemongrass with Thai Chile Salsa

❖

Shrimp Empanadas

❖

Grilled Quail with Mole Sauce

APPETIZERS

*P*erhaps the most important contribution made to American food customs in the 1980s was the "grazing" phenomenon. That's industry jargon for doing what the Mexicans and Spanish have been doing for centuries: eating small plates called *antojitos* and tapas.

The working class in most traditional cultures would eat their big meal in the middle of the long working day. The agrarian Hispano families of northern New Mexico followed this practice, concluding the day with a simple supper bowl of *atole*, a gruel made from toasted blue cornmeal, with perhaps a small plate of greens alongside. I find myself tending toward this healthier regimen. When I go out to a restaurant for dinner, I often order two appetizers in lieu of a starter and a heavier main plate. This gives me the chance to range around the menu—to "graze"—tasting small amounts of different foods.

When you travel to Mexico, don't miss the vendor food at the open-air markets and on the beaches. These are light meals quite unlike American snack and junk foods. A juicy ripe yellow mango on a stick at the produce market, or sesame-seed candies from a sidewalk seller in Oaxaca will be truly refreshing, delicious, and satisfying.

If you travel to Spain, be sure to go to the tapas bars where little plates are a way of life. Roving the streets of Madrid or Seville—or any city or village in Spain—in pursuit of the best tapas is a worthy culinary pursuit. Ask the barkeep what the house specialty is, because every bar has its forte. You will know instantly if there is a good cook in the kitchen by tasting one or two of the offerings.

I have tried to build versatility into the appetizer recipes that follow. For instance, the recipe for quail can be doubled and served with greens to make a dinner or a delightful cold picnic lunch. The empanadas can be made large or small. The corn cakes make great bite-sized appetizers when formed silver-dollar size and served with a dollop of *queso blanco* and a sprinkle of *calabacitas* on top. Or you can make them as large as a folded omelet and serve them for breakfast, lunch, or dinner.

Appetizers are meant to stimulate the appetite and to be a promise of what is to come.

Whole Roasted Garlic with Asadero or Brie Cheese and Tomatillo-Cilantro Salsa

*O*ften requested by our patrons, this simple yet sumptuous recipe is a United Nations plate. The whole roasted garlic is a staple Italian dish, the *asadero* is a contemporary melt-away white Mexican cheese, and the salsa is from Old Mexico. Or you can choose to put France on the plate by using Brie in place of the *asadero.*

Thanks go to my brother Peter for this dish. On *seven* different occasions he sent me the menu from his favorite Italian restaurant in San Francisco with the roasted garlic offering circled. Finally, I developed this appetizer, and have been grateful to him ever since! Set out oyster forks for the guests to use to lift the roasted garlic cloves whole from their skins. The cloves will spread like softened butter on a piece of French bread or warmed flour tortilla. Also, out of respect for Peter's abhorrence of cilantro, please note that Italian flat-leaf parsley may be substituted for the cilantro in the salsa.

Serves 4

4 whole bulbs garlic

1/4 cup olive oil

For the tomatillo-cilantro salsa:

1/3 pound tomatillos, husks removed

1/2 small white onion, chopped

1 clove garlic

1 fresh *serrano* chile, stemmed

1/4 cup water

1/2 teaspoon salt

1/2 bunch fresh cilantro (coriander) or flat-leaf parsley, stemmed

6 ounces *asadero* cheese or Brie cheese, cut into 4 equal pieces

1 loaf French bread, sliced, or 12 white-flour or whole-wheat tortillas, warmed

Preheat an oven to 375° F.

To prepare the garlic bulbs for roasting, remove the excess papery skin but leave the bulbs whole. Cut off the top 1/2 inch of each bulb, exposing the tops of the individual garlic cloves. If some of the clove tops remain uncut, take a little slice off each with a paring knife to expose the inside.

Place the garlic bulbs, cut sides up, in a deep-sided casserole or loaf pan and add water to reach ≋

halfway up the sides of the bulbs. Drizzle the olive oil evenly over the tops of the bulbs. Cover tightly with aluminum foil and place in the oven. Bake until the cloves feel soft when pressed, about 1 hour.

Meanwhile, prepare the salsa. Place the tomatillos, onion, garlic, chile, and water in a blender or a food processor fitted with the metal blade. Add the cilantro or parsley and whirl until smooth. Do not add the cilantro or parsley until just before serving because it will lose its flavor and bright green color. You will have about 3/4 cup salsa.

To serve, preheat a broiler. Place 1 piece of the cheese on each of 4 flameproof serving plates. Run the plates under the broiler until the cheese just begins to melt, 3 to 5 minutes. Be careful not to allow the cheese to melt into a puddle. Place a garlic bulb next to the cheese and flood the plate with the salsa. Accompany with French bread or tortillas.

CORN CAKES WITH CALABACITAS AND QUESO BLANCO SALSA

his dish is beloved by our vegetarian and nonvegetarian patrons alike. I was inspired to create it in order to offer the centuries-old *calabacitas*, the Southwest's classic corn and squash sauté. The white cheese salsa is essentially the *chile con queso* of Old Mexico, but made with ingredients available north of the border. These corn cakes may be served as an appetizer or as a lunch or brunch main course.

Serves 6

For the *queso blanco salsa*:

1/4 cup unsalted butter

1 white onion, chopped

5 Italian plum tomatoes, peeled and chopped

4 fresh mild green chiles such as New Mexico or Anaheim, roasted, seeded, peeled, and chopped (page 22; see note)

1 red bell pepper, seeded, deveined, and diced

1 yellow bell pepper, seeded, deveined, and diced

1/4 teaspoon salt

1/4 teaspoon freshly ground black pepper

1/2 cup half-and-half

1/2 pound cream cheese, cut into small pieces

1/2 teaspoon cayenne pepper

For the corn cakes:

1/3 cup finely diced red bell pepper

1 cup fresh or thawed, frozen corn kernels

3 eggs

3/4 cup milk

1/2 cup all-purpose flour

1/3 cup stone-ground yellow cornmeal

2 tablespoons unsalted butter, melted and cooled

1 teaspoon salt

2 dashes of Tabasco sauce

1/2 to 1 teaspoon cayenne pepper

1/4 cup finely minced scallions, including the green tops

1/4 cup stemmed fresh cilantro (coriander) leaves, chopped

3 tablespoons freshly grated Parmesan cheese

Melted butter for cooking

For the *calabacitas*:

2 tablespoons butter, melted

**2 cups fresh or thawed, frozen corn
    kernels**

1 cup finely diced red bell pepper

1 cup finely diced zucchini

**2 fresh *poblano* chiles, stemmed,
    seeded, and finely chopped**

**Fresh cilantro (coriander) sprigs for
    garnish**

To prepare the salsa, melt the butter in a large sauté pan over medium heat. When the butter sizzles, add the onion and sauté until translucent, about 7 minutes. Add the tomatoes, chiles, red and yellow bell peppers, salt, and black pepper. Cook for 10 minutes, stirring frequently.

Reduce the heat and add the half-and-half, stirring well. When heated through, add the cream cheese. Cook, stirring frequently, until the cheese melts and the mixture is thick, about 12 minutes. Stir in the cayenne pepper and remove from the heat. Let cool, cover, and refrigerate until 30 minutes before serving. (You may prepare the salsa up to 3 days in advance.)

Just before serving, reheat the salsa by placing it in the top pan of a double boiler over gently simmering water; stir frequently to prevent scorching. Adjust to taste with cayenne pepper.

To prepare the corn cake batter, combine the bell pepper, corn, eggs, milk, flour, cornmeal, butter, and salt in a blender or in a food processor fitted with the metal blade. Process for about 30 seconds. Transfer the mixture to a large bowl, and stir in the

Tabasco sauce, cayenne pepper, scallions, cilantro, and Parmesan cheese. Cover and let stand for 30 minutes at room temperature.

Preheat an oven to 250° F.

To cook the corn cakes, warm a 7-inch nonstick sauté pan over medium heat until hot. Brush the pan with melted butter. When the butter sizzles, ladle 3 or 4 tablespoons of batter into the center of the pan, then tilt and swirl the pan to spread the batter thinly over the pan's surface. Cook until lightly browned on the bottom, about 2 minutes. Flip the cake and cook until the second side browns slightly, another minute. Slide the cake out onto a plate and cover with waxed paper. Make 6 cakes in all in this manner, brushing the pan with butter as needed. As the cakes are cooked, stack them, slipping a sheet of waxed paper between them to prevent sticking, and place in the oven to keep warm until serving. They may be cooked up to 1 hour ahead of serving.

To prepare the *calabacitas*, warm a sauté pan over medium heat until hot. Brush the pan with the melted butter. When it sizzles, add all the remaining ingredients. Cook, shaking the pan to rearrange the ingredients frequently, until the vegetables are just heated through and slightly softened, 3 to 4 minutes.

To assemble, place the corn cakes on individual plates and divide the *calabacitas* evenly among them, spooning it on one-half of each corn cake. Fold the other half over to form a half-moon. Ladle the warm salsa over all. Garnish with cilantro sprigs.

Note: Canned green chiles may be used in place of the fresh; be sure to rinse them with water before adding to the salsa.

OAXACAN MANGOES

Mangoes are unequivocally my favorite food! I adapted this recipe from the succulent "walk-away" mangoes sold by vendors in the open-air market of Oaxaca in southern Mexico. The mangoes are peeled and cut like a giant radish flower and sold impaled whole on a stick. A salsa of chile powder, salt, and lime and orange juices is poured over the mango. Mexican markets are a paradise for cooks. To wander the stalls while biting into one of these sweet, cool mangoes is an unparalleled treat.

At Cafe Pasqual's we cut mangoes in half and then cut the halves to resemble the bristles of a porcupine. The sculpted surface captures a juicy salsa in its crevices. This fancy presentation was taught to me by my dear friend chef Marcello Lynd. The recipe works equally well as a dessert offering.

Serves 4

For the salsa:

1/2 cup fresh orange juice

1/4 cup fresh lime juice

2 teaspoons kosher salt

3/4 teaspoon cayenne pepper

**1 teaspoon Chimayó chile powder
  (optional)**

Dash of Tabasco sauce

4 just ripe mangoes

1 lime, cut into 4 wedges, for garnish

4 fresh mint sprigs for garnish

To make the salsa, in a small bowl stir together all the ingredients until well mixed.

To prepare each mango, stand it on end, stem end up, with a narrow side facing you. Slice straight down 1 inch away from either side of the stem. (The bit of fruit left clinging to the pit is strictly for the cook, to be eaten while leaning over the sink.) You now have 2 halves.

With a mango half in the palm of your hand, cut side up, score the flesh with the tip of a sharp paring knife, making a diagonal 1/2-inch grid. Take care to cut through the flesh deeply, but not through the skin. Repeat with the second half.

Now, press against the side of each half so the cut flesh pops upward, to create a porcupine effect. Repeat with the remaining mangoes.

Serve the halves overlapping on individual plates. Spoon the prepared salsa over all, and garnish with the lime wedges and mint sprigs.

Note: For a buffet, arrange prepared mango halves on a large platter, scatter lime wedges over all, and decorate with small triangles of watermelon with the rind still on, to be eaten as finger food.

My favorite mango variety is the Haden. It is small and reddish, and the flesh is deeper orange and more flavorful than the more commonly found Tommy Atkins variety. The Tommy Atkins mango is larger and weighs nearly a pound. It has a speckled, light, gold-yellow skin and flesh. A ripe mango will yield to pressure when pinched and have a sweet fragrance emanating from the stem.

Steamed Mussels with Thai Basil and Lemongrass with Thai Chile Salsa

Contributed by chef Laura Taylor, this unforgettable appetite whetter was one she recorded on her travels in Thailand one year. We missed her that winter, but she consoled us by sending us this masterpiece in the middle of her holiday. Thai basil is found fresh in Asian markets along with lemongrass, dried leaves from the kaffir lime tree, and Thai chiles. If you cannot find the Thai basil, use the leaves from 3 sprigs of basil along with the leaves from 1 stalk of fresh mint.

Serves 6

For the Thai chile salsa:

4 to 6 fresh Thai chiles, stemmed and finely minced

1 tablespoon finely chopped, peeled fresh ginger

1 tablespoon finely minced garlic

2 Italian plum tomatoes, finely diced

1/3 cup fresh lime juice

1/2 cup water

1 tablespoon Thai fish sauce

2 teaspoons granulated sugar

1/4 cup fresh cilantro (coriander) leaves, finely chopped

For the steamed mussels:

3 pounds mussels in the shell

2 tablespoons cornmeal

3 lemongrass stalks, cut into 1-inch lengths

8 kaffir lime leaves

4 shallots, quartered

8 cloves garlic, sautéed whole in their skins

1 bunch fresh Thai basil, stemmed

4-inch piece fresh ginger, unpeeled, cut on the diagonal into slices 1/8 inch thick

To prepare the salsa, in a small bowl stir together all the ingredients. Adjust the "heat" of the salsa to taste by adjusting the amount of chiles. If not serving the salsa immediately, set it aside, but for no more than 2 hours.

Mussels are marketed alive in their shells. To prepare the mussels, place them in a large bowl, add water to cover, and then add the cornmeal. Let them soak for about 1 hour. The mussels will ingest the cornmeal, and then spit it out, a process that flushes the meat of any grit. Drain the mussels, scrub them well, and remove their beards. Discard any mussels that are open or cracked. ≈

Place the mussels and all the remaining ingredients for steaming in a large pot. Add water to cover by 1 inch. Cover and steam over high heat until the mussels open, 7 to 15 minutes.

Serve the mussels in shallow individual bowls. Place the salsa in small bowls alongside for dipping.

Note: If you have a stone mortar and pestle, by all means use them for making the salsa for this recipe; the flavors will marry beautifully!

Chef Laura Taylor, Cafe Pasqual's.

SHRIMP EMPANADAS

*E*mpanadas are turnovers. The savory empanadas we offer are the creation of chef Sally Witham and are an interesting twist on what are customarily meat-filled pies. Use lard for authentic flavor and superb flakiness, or substitute solid vegetable shortening for a more health-conscious alternative. The empanadas can be assembled four hours before serving, but be sure to refrigerate them if you do. These are rich appetizers, so easy does it on the main course.

Makes 12 empanadas; serves 6

For the empanada dough:

3 1/4 cups all-purpose flour

1/2 cup (1/4 pound) lard, chilled

1/2 cup (1/4 pound) butter, chilled

1 1/2 teaspoons salt

1/2 cup ice water

For the empanada filling:

3 tablespoons medium-hot red pepper
   flakes

1 lemon, halved

1/2 pound shrimp, peeled and deveined

3/4 cup Black Beans, well drained
   (page 38)

2 cups grated Monterey Jack cheese

3 tablespoons Chimayó chile powder

1 egg

1/2 tablespoon water

1 1/2 cups Tomatillo-Cilantro Salsa
   (pages 104–5)

3 to 4 cups peanut oil for frying

To prepare the dough, place the flour in a large bowl. Cut the lard and butter into walnut-size pieces and work it into the flour with your fingertips until the mixture is well blended and has the consistency of dry oatmeal.

In a cup or small bowl, dissolve the salt in the ice water. Slowly pour the water into the flour mixture, stirring with a wooden spoon as you do. The dough will start to pull away from the sides of the bowl and will easily form a ball that is soft and malleable. Put the dough in plastic wrap and chill for at least 1 hour.

To prepare the filling, place enough water in a large saucepan to cover the shrimp once they are added. Add the pepper flakes and lemon and bring to a boil over high heat. When boiling, add the shrimp. Cover and cook until the shrimp just turn pink, 2 to 3 minutes. Drain the shrimp, rinse off any stray pepper flakes, and discard the lemon halves.

Cut the shrimp into quarters by halving them lengthwise and then horizontally. Place in a mixing bowl and let cool to room temperature. Add the ≈

beans, cheese, and chile powder. Toss lightly to combine. Set aside.

Place the chilled dough on a clean, dry surface sprinkled with a little flour. Roll out 1/4 inch thick. Using the rim of a bowl as a cutter, cut out dough rounds 4 inches in diameter. This amount of dough will easily make 12 rounds.

To assemble the empanadas, break the egg into a small bowl, add the water, and beat together with a fork. Brush the perimeter of each dough round with the egg wash. Place 2 tablespoons of the shrimp mixture, slightly pressed together, on one side of each dough round. Fold each round in half to create a half-moon. Gently press the outer edges of the dough together using the tines of a fork, and prick the top of each empanada 2 or 3 times. As the empanadas are made, place them on a baking sheet. When all of them are assembled, chill for 1 hour before frying.

Prepare the salsa as directed, up to the point where the cilantro is added. You will need to double the recipe in order to yield enough for this dish. Add the cilantro and finish the salsa just before serving.

To fry the empanadas, heat the peanut oil in a deep-sided stockpot to 370° F, or until a pinch of raw dough dropped into the oil bobs to the surface immediately. Another test for frying temperature is to insert the handle of a wooden spoon into the oil. If small bubbles immediately form around the handle, the oil is hot enough to use.

Place an empanada in a flat strainer or slotted spoon and gently lower it into the hot oil. If the oil sizzles a lot and the empanada browns very quickly, reduce the heat a little before continuing. Cook the empanadas, one or two at a time, until golden brown, 5 to 7 minutes. Using the slotted strainer or spoon, remove them to paper towels to drain.

To serve, arrange 2 empanadas on each individual plate and ladle 1/4 cup of the salsa over all.

GRILLED QUAIL WITH MOLE SAUCE

*T*hese tiny feathered friends are the ideal size to pique the appetite. Serve the golden birds on a plate flooded with *mole* for a stunning beginning. Ask your butcher for boned quail for an easy, elegant presentation.

You may substitute chicken wing "drumsticks" for the quail. To create a drumstick from a chicken wing, cut off the upper wing and loosen the tendons attached at the "handle" end of the wing. Using a sharp paring knife, start at the handle end of the wing and scrape the meat down to the other end to form a ball of chicken meat. The wing now resembles a drumstick.

The *mole* recipe yields a generous amount. Plan to serve this special quail dish when you already have some *mole* on hand.

Serves 6

6 whole quail, boned

1 cup olive oil

2 tablespoons minced garlic

2 tablespoons sesame seeds

3 cups *Mole* (pages 128–29)

Place the quail in a shallow glass bowl. Add the olive oil and garlic and turn the birds to coat completely. Cover and refrigerate for 2 hours.

Prepare a fire in a charcoal grill.

Place the sesame seeds in a small, dry sauté pan over low heat. Toast, stirring frequently, until the seeds are light gold, about 10 minutes. Remove from the heat and let cool.

Arrange the quail on the grill rack about 6 inches above medium-hot coals. Grill, turning once or twice, until the quail are golden brown on all sides, 3 to 5 minutes on each side.

Meanwhile, gently reheat the *mole*, stirring frequently to prevent scorching.

To serve, spoon 1/4 cup *mole* onto each of 6 individual plates. Place a quail on each pool of *mole* and spoon another 1/4 cup *mole* over each quail. Scatter the sesame seeds over the top. Serve immediately.

Summer in the yard, Santa Fe, New Mexico.

GRILLED CHIPOTLE SHRIMP TOSTADAS

❖

PAN-SEARED SALMON WITH ROASTED CUMIN-
CORIANDER CREMA AND CHIPOTLE SALSA

❖

THAI SHRIMP WITH LEMONGRASS-COCONUT
SAUCE AND SCALLION CAKES

❖

POLLO PIBIL WITH SAFFRON RICE AND
FIRE-ROASTED BALSAMIC-MARINATED VEGETABLES

❖

CHICKEN MOLE PRESCILIANO

❖

POLENTA WITH MASCARPONE AND GRILLED
PORTABELLO MUSHROOMS IN TOMATO SAUCE

❖

GRILLED CHIMAYÓ CHILE–RUBBED NEW YORK
STEAK WITH SERRANO MAYONNAISE
AND POTATO-CHIVE CAKES WITHAM

❖

LEG OF LAMB
REDOLENT OF GARLIC AND ROSEMARY

DINNER

*D*inner is an intimate meal. There's time to relax, converse, and savor special food. We set up the cafe in the evening so all these lovely things can happen. The copper shades are lowered, fresh white cloths are laid on the tables, the lights are turned down, and the candles are lit, their flickering light illuminating the lofty ceilings and richly toned wall paintings. Reservations are taken to assure a relaxed atmosphere.

At dinner the menu changes completely. To create each evening's specials we scour the markets and talk with our purveyors. Not being wedded to a particular regional menu, our chef is free to choose from among the very best of what the season offers. Vegetables, meats, and seafoods are prepared to their advantage, revealing their intrinsic qualities, simply. Those who work in the kitchen consider shaping the dinner menu a thrilling opportunity and a privilege.

Out of the specials are born meals destined to become classics. The goal is to make our worlds larger, to awaken our senses in the celebration of food and wine. For the diner that means a new dining experience. For the cooks that means perhaps a new addition to the repertoire.

In our increasingly fast-paced culture, where time is of the essence, a leisurely meal and convivial company and conversation are nearly forgotten pastimes. It is no wonder that some people think eating has become a chore. But a simple dinner with old or new friends, face to face at a table, can establish or restore communication and intimacy, and perhaps bring about cherished memories.

It is my hope that these recipes will help to create such moments in your life. The dinner recipes presented here can easily be accomplished at home. May they bring pleasure to your table.

GRILLED CHIPOTLE SHRIMP TOSTADAS

*C*hipotles are dry-smoked jalapeño chiles. Sometimes they are canned in *adobo* sauce. The chiles have an unparalleled woodsy taste. *Queso ranchero* is a dry Mexican goat cheese and is the best cheese to use for this dish. If it is unavailable, substitute the saltier, but wonderfully textured feta cheese. This extremely popular dish is the invention of chef Laura Taylor and reflects her unique, kicky nature.

Use a spice mill or coffee grinder to grind *chipotles*, removing their stems first. If you are using the *chipotle morita* it may be too pliable to grind. Use a sharp knife to chop it into small bits.

Serves 4

2 tablespoons *chipotle* chile powder
   (about 6 chiles)

1/3 cup Chimayó chile powder

1 tablespoon kosher salt

24 large shrimp, peeled and deveined

3/4 cup olive oil

8 fresh cilantro (coriander) or flat-leaf
   parsley sprigs

For the refried black beans:

1½ teaspoons cumin seeds

1½ teaspoons coriander seeds

1½ tablespoons Chimayó chile powder

3/4 cup olive oil

3 cups Black Beans with their liquid
   (page 38) or canned black beans
   with their liquid

Salt

For the tortillas:

2 cups peanut oil

8 blue corn or yellow corn tortillas

For the salsa:

4 ripe Italian plum tomatoes

2 tomatillos, husks removed

1/2 avocado, peeled

1/4 red onion

1 fresh jalapeño chile, stemmed

3/4 cup fresh orange juice

1 tablespoon fresh lime juice

1 tablespoon olive oil

Salt

3/4 cup crumbled *queso ranchero* or
   feta cheese (3 ounces)

8 fresh cilantro (coriander) or flat-leaf
   parsley sprigs for garnish

In a small bowl, stir together both chile powders and the salt. Dip the shrimp into the mixture, coating well on all sides. Place the coated shrimp in a shallow pan and pour the olive oil evenly over all. (Discard any chile coating that remains, as contamination could result from its later use.) Cover the shrimp and marinate in the refrigerator while you prepare the beans and tortillas.

Prepare a fire in a charcoal grill. Preheat an oven to 250° F.

To prepare the beans, combine the cumin and coriander seeds and the chile powder in a small, dry sauté pan over medium heat. Roast until the aromas are released, about 2 minutes. Remove from the heat and let cool. Place the spices in a spice mill or coffee grinder and grind until pulverized. Alternatively, pulverize in a mortar using a pestle.

Warm the olive oil in a large cast-iron skillet over low heat. Add the beans and ground roasted spices and cook, mashing the beans with the back of a wooden spoon and stirring frequently. Adjust to taste with salt. Continue to cook until the beans absorb the oil and flavors, about 10 minutes. Set aside, covered, in the oven until time to assemble the tostadas.

To ready the tortillas, heat the peanut oil in a skillet large enough to accommodate the tortillas laid flat, one at a time. When the oil is hot but not smoking, using tongs grasp a tortilla and slip it into the hot oil. Fry until crisp but not brown, about 2 minutes. It will curl up somewhat on the edges. Remove to paper towels to drain and reserve in the warm oven until time to assemble the tostadas. Repeat with the remaining tortillas.

To prepare the salsa, cut the tomatoes, tomatillos, avocado, onion, and jalapeño into 1/4-inch dice. Place in a bowl and stir in the citrus juices and oil. Season to taste with salt.

Just before serving time, using tongs arrange the shrimp on the grill rack. Alternatively, skewer the shrimp on 2 parallel bamboo skewers for easy turning. Grill quickly until pink and cooked through, 2 to 3 minutes on each side.

To serve, place 2 fried tortillas on each individual plate. Place about 1/3 cup refried beans in the center of each tortilla. Arrange 3 grilled shrimp on top of each mound of beans. Spoon the salsa over and around the shrimp, using all of the salsa. Sprinkle the crumbled cheese over the top and garnish with cilantro or parsley sprigs. Serve immediately.

A roadside produce stand, Española, New Mexico.

PAN-SEARED SALMON WITH ROASTED CUMIN-CORIANDER CREMA AND CHIPOTLE SALSA

Chef Jason Aufrichtig created this light treatment for rich salmon. When purchasing the salmon, ask for fillets not steaks. The chile in *adobo* that is called for in the salsa is a canned product, sold at Latino groceries. The chiles keep for weeks in the refrigerator if they are first transferred to a nonreactive container. They are packed in a red chile sauce, to which vinegar has been added, and are very piquant. There is no substitution for the zippy taste they add to sauces and fillings.

Serves 6

6 salmon fillets with skin intact, 8 ounces each

1 cup fresh oregano leaves, stemmed and finely minced

1 cup fresh basil leaves, stemmed and finely minced

1 1/2 cups fresh parsley leaves, stemmed and finely minced

For the cumin-coriander *crema*:

1 tablespoon plus 3/4 teaspoon cumin seeds

1 tablespoon coriander seeds

1 cup plain low-fat yogurt

2 tablespoons heavy cream

1/2 bunch fresh cilantro (coriander), stemmed and coarsely chopped

2 cloves garlic, finely minced

Juice of 1 lemon

For the *chipotle* salsa:

1 egg

1 teaspoon Chimayó chile powder

1 *chipotle* chile in *adobo*

Juice of 1/2 lemon

1 clove garlic

1 1/4 cups olive oil

1/2 cup olive oil

Rinse and dry each salmon fillet. It is not necessary to remove the skin from the fillets. Check for pinbones by running your fingertips over the flesh side of the fillet. Use pliers or tweezers to remove any bones.

In a small bowl stir together the oregano, basil, and parsley. Pat the herbs onto the flesh side of each fillet, covering well. Refrigerate until ready to cook.

To prepare the *crema*, combine the cumin and coriander seeds in a small, dry sauté pan over medium heat. Roast the seeds, shaking the pan frequently, ≈

until the aromas are released, about 2 minutes. Remove from the heat and let cool. Place the spices in a spice mill or coffee grinder and grind to pulverize the seeds. Alternatively, pulverize in a mortar using a pestle.

In a small bowl, combine the ground seeds with all the remaining *crema* ingredients. Let sit for 30 minutes so the flavors can develop and blend. Pour through a fine-mesh strainer into a bowl to remove the cilantro leaves. You will have about 1 cup. (The *crema* will keep for up to 1 week in the refrigerator.)

To prepare the salsa, place all the ingredients, except the olive oil, in a food processor fitted with the metal blade or in a blender. Blend thoroughly. With the motor running, slowly pour in the olive oil in a thin, steady stream, continuing to process until a mayonnaiselike sauce is achieved. Transfer to a bowl, cover, and refrigerate until serving. You will have about 1¼ cups. (The salsa will keep for up to 2 days in the refrigerator.)

About 15 minutes before serving, place a sauté pan large enough to hold the salmon, with room to spare, over medium heat. Add the olive oil. When the oil is just smoking, put the fillets in the pan, herb sides down. Cook 4 to 5 minutes, then turn and cook on the second side until done, 4 to 5 minutes longer. Cooking times vary according to taste and the thickness of the fillet. At Cafe Pasqual's fish is considered done when the middle is still moist and a bit darker than the surrounding light pink flesh.

To serve, spoon the *crema* onto individual plates, dividing it equally among them. Place 1 salmon fillet on each plate, herbed sides up, to cover half the *crema*. Drizzle the salsa decoratively onto the fillet and then onto the visible half of the *crema*.

Thai Shrimp with Lemongrass-Coconut Sauce and Scallion Cakes

Chef Jason Aufrichtig, inspired by the Thai ingredients in the cafe's pantry, invented the simple, rich sauce we use in this dish. It's a festive bright yellow and easy to prepare for a party or special dinner. We have also served the sauce with cold poached salmon; you can team it up with numerous other creations such as seafood or vegetable pasta dishes. It is definitely worth spending the time to gather the ingredients.

Serves 6

For the lemongrass-coconut sauce:

3 stalks lemongrass, sliced into thin rounds

4 cloves garlic, minced

3 fresh *serrano* chiles, stemmed and finely minced

4 fresh Thai chiles

3/4 cup minced, peeled fresh ginger

4 kaffir lime leaves

2 cans (13 1/2 ounces each) unsweetened coconut milk

3 cups heavy cream

1 tablespoon ground turmeric

1/4 cup Thai fish sauce

For the scallion cakes:

3 cups peanut oil

12 whole-wheat tortillas

2 eggs, beaten

6 tablespoons Asian sesame oil

1 cup finely sliced scallions, including the green tops

For the shrimp:

2 to 4 tablespoons olive oil

2 1/2 pounds large shrimp (about 30), peeled and deveined

6 large fresh cilantro (coriander) sprigs for garnish

To prepare the sauce, combine all the ingredients in a saucepan over medium heat. Simmer gently, stirring occasionally, until the sauce is reduced by one-fifth, about 40 minutes.

To prepare the scallion cakes, preheat an oven to 250° F. Warm the peanut oil in a large, shallow skillet over high heat. While the oil is heating, brush 6 tortillas on one side only with the beaten egg. Spoon 1 tablespoon of the sesame oil onto each of these tortillas and then sprinkle evenly with the scallions. ≈

Brush the remaining 6 tortillas on one side only with beaten egg and place them on top of the prepared tortillas, egg side in, to form 6 "cakes." Pass a rolling pin across each cake to press the layers together.

To determine when the oil is ready to fry the cakes, tear off a tiny bit of tortilla and slip it into the nearly smoking oil. When it bobs quickly to the surface, the oil is ready. Another test for readiness is to plunge a wooden spoon or chopstick into the hot oil. If tiny bubbles coalesce immediately around the wood, the oil is ready.

Carefully, to avoid dangerous splashing, slide 1 cake into the hot oil. Take care to submerge the cake. It will puff after a few moments. Using tongs, turn the cake, taking care to submerge it again. When golden and crisp but not too dark, after about 3 minutes, raise the cake and drain it over the oil, then transfer it to paper towels to drain.

Repeat with the remaining cakes. Work carefully but quickly. Slip the finished cakes into the oven to keep warm. When all the cakes are fried, using a sharp, heavy knife or, ideally, a Chinese cleaver, cut each cake into 8 wedges.

To cook the shrimp, heat the olive oil in a sauté pan. Add the shrimp and sauté 1 to 2 minutes per side. Drain off excess oil. Add the sauce and heat through for 1 minute before serving.

To serve, allow 1 cake per serving. Place the sautéed shrimp on 4 of the scallion cake sections and top with the sauce. Keep 4 pieces of the scallion cake to the side of the plate as a crisp accompaniment. Garnish with the cilantro sprigs.

Note: You may want to serve the shrimp over bean-thread noodles or rice and serve the scallion cakes on the side. Cook the bean-thread noodles in boiling water to cover until soft, about 5 minutes, then drain. Rice may be cooked according to a favorite recipe.

POLLO PIBIL WITH SAFFRON RICE AND FIRE-ROASTED BALSAMIC-MARINATED VEGETABLES

*T*his extraordinary grilled chicken dish was given to me by Daniel Stevens, a dear old friend. It has been part of our menu from the moment I tasted it. In the Yucatán, where it is a traditional dish, the chicken is enveloped in banana leaves, buried in a pit called a *pibil*, and steamed—hence, *pollo* ("chicken") *pibil* ("pit roasted"). At Cafe Pasqual's we charcoal-grill the chicken breasts and serve them with bright yellow saffron rice and colorful marinated vegetables. The *achiote*, a paste of dried *annatto* seeds, is a sweet, earthy counterpoint to the citrus and garlic flavors. Be sure to allow plenty of time for marinating the chicken well; 24 hours is best.

Serves 6

For the chicken:

4 teaspoons cumin seeds

1 Mexican cinnamon stick, about
     3 inches

1 teaspoon whole cloves

1½ tablespoons whole black
     peppercorns

1/2 cup *achiote* paste

3 tablespoons kosher salt

2 tablespoons finely minced garlic

2 cups fresh orange juice

1/2 cup fresh lime juice

2 tablespoons stemmed fresh marjoram
     leaves, or 1 tablespoon dried
     marjoram leaves

1/2 cup olive oil

6 chicken breasts halves

For the balsamic-marinated vegetables:

1 cup olive oil

1/3 cup balsamic vinegar

1 tablespoon minced garlic

2 teaspoons freshly ground black
     pepper

Kosher salt

1 large red onion, sliced into thick
     rounds

2 red bell peppers, seeded, deveined,
     and cut into long strips 1/2 inch
     wide

2 yellow squash, sliced lengthwise into
     1/4-inch-wide slabs

2 zucchini, sliced lengthwise into
     1/4-inch-wide slabs

2 Japanese eggplants, sliced lengthwise
     into 1/4-inch-wide slabs

For the saffron rice:

1 teaspoon saffron threads

1/4 cup olive oil

1/2 white onion, finely minced

2 teaspoons finely minced garlic

1 1/2 teaspoons kosher salt

1/2 teaspoon white pepper

2 cups long-grain white rice

3 cups water

To prepare the chicken, combine the cumin, cinnamon, and cloves in a small, dry sauté pan over medium heat. Roast, shaking the pan frequently, until the aromas are released, about 2 minutes. Remove from the heat and let cool. Place the spices in a spice mill or coffee grinder and grind until pulverized. Alternatively, pulverize in a mortar using a pestle.

Combine all the remaining ingredients, except the chicken, in a blender or in a food processor fitted with the metal blade. Process just long enough to incorporate.

Put the chicken breasts in a shallow glass dish. Pour the spice mixture evenly over the top to cover completely. Cover and place in the refrigerator to marinate for at least 24 hours or up to 36 hours, turning frequently.

To prepare the marinade for the vegetables, in a bowl stir together the olive oil, vinegar, garlic, pepper, and salt to taste. Put all of the sliced vegetables in a shallow glass bowl and pour the marinade evenly over the top to coat each piece well. Marinate at room temperature for 4 to 6 hours.

Prepare a fire in a charcoal grill.

To prepare the rice, place the saffron in a small, dry sauté pan over medium heat. Toast, continuously shaking the pan to prevent scorching, until fragrant, about 2 minutes. Remove from the heat and reserve.

Combine the olive oil, onion, garlic, salt, and white pepper in the bottom of a large saucepan over medium heat. Stir for 1 to 2 minutes, then add the rice. Stir constantly until the oil is absorbed and the rice begins to smell nutty, 1 to 2 minutes longer.

Add the water to the rice mixture, making sure that all the grains of rice are submerged and the rice is evenly distributed on the bottom of the pan. Then, add the toasted saffron and bring to a boil over medium-high heat. Reduce the heat to low, cover, and simmer until all the water is absorbed, 20 to 30 minutes.

Remove the chicken breasts from the marinade. Arrange the breasts, skin sides down, on the grill rack about 6 inches above medium-hot coals. Grill, being careful not to overcook; this recipe should yield juicy chicken. Turn the breasts once during cooking. The cooking time depends upon the heat of the coals, the thickness of the breasts, and other variables. Plan on 15 to 20 minutes' total grilling time.

Between 5 and 10 minutes before the chicken is ready, add the marinated vegetables to the grill rack. Grill, turning frequently, until charred, 7 to 12 minutes.

Remove the chicken and vegetables from the grill and serve hot with saffron rice.

Hornos, *outdoor ovens used for baking bread and drying corn, Velarde, New Mexico.*

CHICKEN MOLE PRESCILIANO

*M*ole is an ancient Aztec dish made with dried red chiles, fruits, nuts, vegetables, spices, seeds, and, yes, chocolate. It is very rich, complex in flavor, and deeply satisfying. This Puebla-style *mole* is the family recipe of Presciliano Ruiz, who has been our revered and celebrated cook for many years. It is unusual in that it does not contain lard! It may be refrigerated for up to ten days and it freezes beautifully for up to two months. I keep *mole* in the freezer for unexpected guests; it's quick to reheat and makes a delicious and satisfying quick meal. As this recipe is involved, and requires an investment of time, it has been written to guarantee a quantity will be left over.

Serve the chicken with Guacamole (page 42), warmed corn tortillas, and cold Mexican beer.

Makes 4 quarts sauce; serves 4 to 6 with enough sauce for 1 or 2 more dinners

For the *mole*:

4 *chipotle* chiles

16 *ancho* chiles or *mulato* chiles

16 *pasilla negro* chiles

1 large red bell pepper

1 1/4 cups (5 ounces) sesame seeds

1 1/3 cups peanut oil

1/3 loaf French bread, sliced

1 cup walnut pieces

1 tablet (3 ounces) Mexican chocolate

1 Mexican cinnamon stick, about 3 inches long

2 Italian plum tomatoes

4 cloves garlic

4 tomatillos, husks removed

1 ripe banana, peeled and cut into chunks

3-inch piece (1 1/2 ounces) fresh ginger, sliced in 1/2-inch-thick rounds

1/2 large white onion, quartered

4 quarts water

2 cups olive oil

1 to 2 cups brown sugar (optional)

1 1/2 chickens

Preheat an oven to 350° F.

Clean any dust and dirt from the dried chiles with a damp towel and dry them off thoroughly. If the chiles are moist during the dry sautéing, they will char and be bitter. Stem all the chiles but do not seed. Set aside.

Roast the red bell pepper (page 22), then stem and peel but do not seed. Set aside.

Place the sesame seeds in a dry 10-inch sauté pan over low heat. Stir the seeds or shake the pan constantly until the seeds are slightly brown, ≈

20 to 25 minutes. Be careful not to burn them. Remove from the heat and empty into a good-sized bowl to cool. Reserve 3 tablespoons of the browned seeds for garnish.

In a large, dry sauté pan over low heat, place the *chipotle*, *ancho* or *mulato*, and *pasilla negro* chiles. Shake the pan constantly or stir the chiles until they are evenly toasted, 3 to 5 minutes. Do not char the dried chiles when toasting them or they will be bitter. Remove the toasted chiles from the pan and set aside.

Pour the peanut oil into the same pan and place over medium heat until hot. Carefully drop in the toasted chiles, a few at a time, and leave each batch in the oil for a few seconds. The chiles should soften, swell, and smell fragrant. Using a slotted utensil, remove the chiles and add them to the toasted sesame seeds. When all of the chiles have been fried, add the bell peppers to the bowl. Reserve the oil, keeping it in the sauté pan.

Place the bread and walnuts on a baking sheet in a single layer. Place in the oven until the bread is dry and the walnuts are lightly toasted, 10 to 15 minutes. Stir the walnuts occasionally so they do not burn.

Meanwhile, break the chocolate tablet and cinnamon stick into 3 or 4 large pieces and place in the bottom of a large bowl. When the toasted walnuts and warm bread are ready, slide them atop the chocolate, to melt it. Set aside.

Reheat the reserved peanut oil in the sauté pan over medium heat. When the oil is hot, add the whole tomatoes, garlic cloves, tomatillos, banana chunks, ginger, and onion. Cook until the onion is translucent, the tomatoes begin to char and burst, and the tomatillos have turned a darker green, 7 to 10 minutes. Empty the contents into a colander to drain. Discard the oil.

Add the drained vegetable mixture to the large bowl containing the chocolate-bread mixture and stir well. Working in batches, transfer the mixture to a blender, and blend, adding enough water to make the resulting sauce smooth but still thick. The sauce should have the consistency of a milkshake, but not be as thick as tomato paste. A blender is easier to use than a food processor for this work. Continue to blend in batches until all of the water and the vegetable mixture have been combined. Strain through a large-mesh strainer or china cap (conically shaped metal strainer), using the back of a wooden spoon to push the purée through.

In a large stockpot, heat the olive oil until it just begins to smoke. Add the pureé. Be careful! Protect yourself from hot splashes by wearing long sleeves and turning off the flame while adding the purée. Whisk the oil and purée together with a wire balloon whisk until well blended. Turn the heat back on to low and cook, stirring frequently so that the *mole* does not burn, for 20 minutes.

Taste the *mole*. If it is too piquant, slowly add brown sugar until a balance is achieved between piquant and sweet. If the chiles are quite hot, you may find yourself adding quite a lot of sugar! You may also want to add a bit more Mexican chocolate to deepen the flavor. Remove from the heat, but cover to keep hot.

Cut the whole chicken into quarters and the half chicken in half, so that you have 6 pieces in all. Place the pieces in a pot large enough to hold them, plus water to cover them by 6 inches. Bring to a boil and simmer over low heat until cooked through, about 30 minutes. Drain, reserving the cooking liquid for another use.

Put the chicken back into the pot and add 6 cups of the *mole*. Heat slowly until the *mole* is heated through.

To serve, place a piece of chicken on each individual plate and ladle a generous amount of *mole* over it, 1 to 2 cups. Sprinkle the reserved toasted sesame seeds over each serving.

POLENTA WITH MASCARPONE AND GRILLED PORTABELLO MUSHROOMS IN TOMATO SAUCE

A terrific vegetarian dish, this could easily be rounded out to make a dinner with the addition of a small green salad or some steamed greens. This recipe makes a yellow mountain of soft polenta. What comfort food! For superior flavor, try to find a stone-ground cornmeal with the word *polenta* on the package. While you are stalking your wild portabellos in the markets, you should have no trouble finding the polenta. *Mascarpone*, the creamy Italian cheese available in the dairy section of gourmet markets, adds a sweet richness and is absolutely necessary to great polenta.

Serves 4 to 6

For the grilled portabello mushrooms:

4 cloves garlic, minced

2 tablespoons fresh thyme leaves, stemmed

1/2 teaspoon freshly grated nutmeg

1 teaspoon freshly ground black pepper

Juice and zest of 2 lemons

1/3 cup balsamic vinegar

1/2 cup olive oil

6 fresh portabello mushrooms

For the tomato sauce:

2 tablespoons olive oil

2 red bell peppers, roasted, peeled, seeded, and cut into pieces (page 22)

1 red onion, sliced

4 cloves garlic, minced

1/2 cup fresh oregano leaves, stemmed and minced

1/4 cup fresh thyme leaves, stemmed and minced

10 Italian plum tomatoes, cut into quarters

1 cup Merlot or Zinfandel wine

2 bay leaves

1 cup water

Salt and freshly ground black pepper

For the polenta:

8 cups water

3/4 teaspoon saffron threads

2 teaspoons salt

2 cups polenta

1/2 pound *mascarpone* cheese

1 cup freshly grated Asiago or Parmesan cheese

To prepare the mushrooms for grilling, combine the garlic, thyme, nutmeg, pepper, lemon juice, vinegar, and olive oil in a bowl and whisk together well. Add the mushrooms, turning to coat well, and marinate at room temperature for 2 hours.

To prepare the tomato sauce, heat the olive oil in a large, nonreactive sauté pan over medium heat. Add the red peppers, onion, and garlic and sauté until soft, 7 to 10 minutes. Add all the other ingredients including salt and pepper to taste, and cook, uncovered, until reduced by half, 30 to 40 minutes.

Working in batches, transfer the sauce to a blender and purée until smooth. Then pass the purée through a fine-mesh strainer to make the purée as smooth as possible. Season to taste with salt and pepper.

Prepare a fire in a charcoal grill. Crisscross grill racks to form a meshed cooking surface, so the mushrooms do not fall through the grate. Alternatively, lay a piece of well-perforated aluminum foil across a portion of the grill to act as a guard.

To prepare the polenta, place the water in a heavy-bottomed saucepan and add the saffron and salt. Bring to a rolling boil over high heat. Slowly add the polenta, stirring constantly with a wooden spoon. Cook over medium heat, stirring constantly, until the raw taste disappears and the polenta begins to "tear" away from the sides of the saucepan, 10 to 15 minutes. Add the cheeses, stirring well. Keep warm in a covered double boiler over lowest heat.

Reheat the tomato purée in a saucepan and cover to keep warm.

Arrange the mushrooms on the grill rack over the hot coals and grill, turning once, until heated through, 3 to 5 minutes on each side.

To serve, mound the polenta on a large heated platter. Spoon the tomato sauce over all and top with the mushrooms.

Deer Dance, Christmas Day, Tesuque Pueblo, located ten miles north of Santa Fe.

Grilled Chimayó Chile–Rubbed New York Steak with Serrano Mayonnaise and Potato-Chive Cakes Witham

I was raised to believe that making a sauce for, or otherwise adulterating, a steak was a crime. Chef Sally Witham immediately turned that thinking around with this recipe. The mild Chimayó chile powder marries ideally with the char from the grill. The potato-chive pancakes make an unexpected variation on the classic steak and potatoes. In fact, our regulars often request the potato pancakes as a side dish to other entrées they order. The fiery flavor of the *serrano*-flavored mayonnaise can be amplified with the addition of more chile. This makes a fabulous dish for entertaining, since the steak is the only part of the meal requiring last-minute preparation. Consider grilling a rack of lamb instead of steak. To ready the rack of lamb properly, have your butcher cut the feather bone and "French" the ribs. Prepare the lamb following the same directions as for the steak.

Serves 6

For the steaks:

6 New York or rib-eye steaks, 8 ounces each

1 cup Chimayó chile powder

1/2 cup olive oil

For the *serrano* mayonnaise:

5 fresh *serrano* chiles, stemmed, seeded, and roughly chopped

2 tablespoons distilled white vinegar

1/2 bunch fresh cilantro (coriander), stemmed and roughly chopped

1 egg yolk

Juice of 1 lime

1/2 teaspoon kosher salt

1/4 teaspoon freshly ground black pepper

2 cups olive oil (do not use extra-virgin olive oil)

For the potato-chive cakes:

2 whole bulbs garlic

5 medium-large Idaho baking potatoes

1/2 cup grated *manchego* cheese

1 egg

1/4 cup minced fresh chives

Salt and freshly ground black pepper

Butter for frying

To prepare the steaks, pat the chile powder evenly over all sides and place them in a shallow glass ∼

dish. Drizzle the olive oil over all. Cover and marinate in the refrigerator for at least 6 hours or for up to 36 hours.

To prepare the mayonnaise, put all the ingredients, except the olive oil, in a food processor fitted with the metal blade or in a blender. Process thoroughly to a mash consistency. With the motor running, slowly add the olive oil in a thin, steady stream, continuing to process until the mixture thickens and emulsifies. Cover and refrigerate until serving.

To prepare the cakes, trim and roast the whole garlic bulbs as described on pages 104–5. Place the unpeeled potatoes in a saucepan, add water to cover, and bring to a boil. Boil until tender, 25 to 35 minutes; test for doneness by piercing with a fork. Drain the potatoes and let cool until they can be handled. Then grate into a large mixing bowl, skin and all, using the largest holes on a hand-held standing grater.

Squeeze the whole roasted garlic cloves from their skins into the grated potato. Add the cheese, egg, and chives and mix well. Season to taste with the salt and pepper. Form the mixture into 6 cakes each about 1½ inches thick. Cover and refrigerate at least 30 minutes or for up to 24 hours before frying.

Prepare a fire in a charcoal grill. Arrange the steaks on a grill rack over medium-hot coals and grill, turning once, until cooked to desired doneness.

While the steaks are grilling, heat a griddle or large cast-iron skillet until medium-hot. Lightly brush the surface with butter and add the cakes. Fry, turning once, until nicely browned and heated through, 4 to 6 minutes on each side.

Serve the grilled steaks topped with a generous dollop of *serrano* mayonnaise and a potato cake on the side.

Leg of Lamb Redolent of Garlic and Rosemary

*R*emember when a roast was the ubiquitous entrée for the special occasion? This recipe brings back those days of working kitchens filled with heady aromas. Use this recipe to yield the leftovers that go into Green Split Pea Soup with Lamb and Garlic Sausage (page 82). You will need to reserve at least 6 cups of combined gravy, meat, and vegetables from this meal to prepare the soup. Be sure to save the lamb bone!

The lamb generally sold at markets is, unfortunately, not of the best possible quality. Before it reaches the consumer, it has been butchered and then probably frozen in Kryo-vac packaging, thawed, cut, and refrozen in Kryo-vac packaging, yielding a flavorless product. Lamb that has been processed in this way has dark flesh and an odor. Fortunately, superior free-range, corn-finished lamb is becoming more widely available. Happily, we have found fabulous lamb locally at Encino Ranch. Challenge your butcher to find a source for you. This lamb will be bright pink with no odor, indicating freshness, will have fat on the leg indicating that it has been grain-fed, and will be sweetly flavored and delicious.

Serves 8

1 leg of lamb, 6 to 8 pounds

5 cloves garlic, roughly cut into thirds

1 tablespoon salt

1 tablespoon freshly ground black pepper

2 tablespoons fresh rosemary leaves, chopped, or 1 tablespoon dried rosemary

8 baking potatoes, cut into quarters

5 large yellow onions, cut into quarters

8 carrots, peeled and cut into 3-inch lengths

For the gravy:

Pan juices and fat from roasted leg of lamb

4 to 6 tablespoons all-purpose flour

1 to 2 cups milk

Salt and freshly ground black pepper

Preheat an oven to 450° F.

In a large metal roasting pan, place the leg of lamb fat and fleshy side up. To stud the leg with the garlic, using the point of a paring knife, make 15 small X-shaped incisions in the fat sheath of the leg. Insert the garlic pieces into the cuts, burying them. Tuck any remaining garlic in the folds of the meat. Rub the leg with the salt, pepper, and rosemary. ≈

Arrange the prepared vegetables around the roast and place in the oven for 15 minutes. Turn the oven temperature down to 350° F and continue to roast until done to your liking, another 16 minutes per pound for medium-rare.

Transfer the roast and vegetables to a warmed carving platter, reserving the juices and fat in the pan for gravy. Let the roast "rest" for at least 15 minutes before carving. This waiting period allows the juices to be reabsorbed and facilitates carving. While the roast is resting, make the gravy.

To prepare the gravy, put the roasting pan on top of the stove over 2 burners turned to medium heat and begin to heat the juices and fat. As the pan heats up, scrape to loosen any crisp, browned bits from the bottom of the pan to incorporate into the gravy. When the liquid is bubbling, make a roux by gently shaking spoonfuls of the flour over the juices, vigorously and continuously stirring with a wire balloon whisk until all is well incorporated. Cook over medium heat until the mixture becomes slightly browned and nutty in flavor, about 5 minutes. Continuing to stir, slowly add enough milk to achieve the desired consistency for gravy. Season to taste with salt and pepper.

Carve the roast and serve the gravy in a bowl on the side.

Narciso Pérez, sheep rancher, at his Encino Ranch near Vaughn, New Mexico.

LEMON TART WITH PIÑON CRUST

❖

LINDA'S CHOCOLATE TRUFFLE TORTE

❖

RIPE FIGS WITH MARSALA CREAM CARROLL

❖

GARNETS IN BLOOD

❖

SANGRÍA SORBET

❖

MEXICAN CHOCOLATE ICE CREAM

❖

TOASTED PIÑON ICE CREAM

❖

LAVENDER-HONEY ICE CREAM

❖

BIZCOCHITOS

❖

FULL MOON COOKIES

DESSERTS

As my friend the art critic MaLin Wilson says, "Desserts are delicate. Dessert is the prize, the reward." And the prize does not have to be overly sweet. Fresh fruit, spices, delicately perfumed wines are all dessert possibilities.

Once in France I was served green almonds still on their stems, resembling fuzzy cocoons. They were creamy and, oh, so barely almond flavored. The thick, celadon green husk that surrounded the nutmeat was a wonder of tactile delight.

When I lived in Japan I became enamored of the traditional tea candies made from pounded rice or a sweetened bean paste. The candies were sculpted from these pliable materials, and the better candies were delicacies produced with incredible attention to detail. If it were springtime, they might be made into the likeness of an iris with its petals still unfurled. It would be named Purple Water Iris Emerging, like a work of art. Respect for season, color, texture, taste, and presentation would all be evident. These memories remind me that a treat comes in many guises and flavors.

At Cafe Pasqual's we select dessert wines from the rapidly growing selection of offerings of small vintners from France, Australia, and here at home. I urge you to explore this largely uncharted sea of pleasure.

You will find in the desserts that follow names that may sound like they are full-tilt sweet. But look again. There are chile flakes in the Mexican Chocolate Ice Cream and cinnamon in the Piñon Ice Cream. The spicy tones lend flavor without being cloying. I don't know anything more delicately flavored than the Lavender-Honey Ice Cream, and yet it is a satisfying dessert.

LEMON TART WITH PIÑON CRUST

A restaurant's dessert list is incomplete without a citrus offering. Easy to prepare and fun to decorate with fresh blueberries, raspberries, or blackberries, this tart is a true treat. It is a daily offering at Cafe Pasqual's.

Makes one 9-inch tart; serves 8

For the tart shell:

1/2 cup (1/4 pound) plus 2 tablespoons
   unsalted butter, chilled

1/4 cup granulated sugar

2 egg yolks

1 tablespoon ice water

1 teaspoon vanilla extract or almond
   extract

1/2 teaspoon salt

1/2 cup all-purpose flour

1/2 cup toasted piñon nuts, roughly
   chopped

For the lemon filling:

6 lemons

9 eggs

1¾ cups granulated sugar

1¼ cups heavy cream

**Berries, pesticide-free edible flowers
   (see note), or confectioners' sugar
   for garnish**

Preheat an oven to 400° F.

To prepare the tart shell, in a food processor fitted with the metal blade, cream together the butter and sugar. Add the egg yolks, water, vanilla or almond extract, and salt. Pulse the machine only 2 or 3 times to incorporate. Add the flour and process for a few seconds, just until the dough begins to come together. Add the nuts and pulse again just enough to mix and for the dough to gather itself into a ball. Enclose the dough ball in plastic wrap and put in the freezer for 20 minutes.

Pat the chilled dough onto the bottom and sides of a 9-inch fluted tart pan with removable bottom. Line the tart shell with aluminum foil and fill with uncooked rice or beans or commercial pie weights. Place in the oven and bake until lightly browned, about 12 minutes. Gently remove the weights and foil. Let the tart shell cool. The beans or rice can be saved for future use when baking another tart shell.

Reduce the oven temperature to 300° F.

To prepare the filling, grate the zest from the lemons and then juice them. Strain the juice. In a bowl beat together the eggs and sugar until well incorporated. Stir in the cream and lemon zest and juice and pour into the cooled tart shell. Place in the oven and bake until the crust is browned and the filling is set, 40 to 45 minutes. If the edges of the tart begin to brown too much during baking, remove from the oven, cover just the pastry's edge with aluminum foil and return to the oven to finish baking. ≈

Remove from the oven and let cool completely. Slip off the pan sides and place the tart on a flat serving plate. Serve at room temperature or chilled. Just before serving, garnish the tart with berries, edible flowers, or, if you prefer it undecorated, a few shakes of confectioners' sugar.

Note: Edible flowers must be grown without the use of poisonous chemicals. They include, but are not limited to, apple blossom, borage, calendula, corn flower (bachelor button), cimbidium, citrus blossom, dianthus, hollyhock, honeysuckle, lilac, marigold, nasturtium, pansy, petunia, rose, snapdragon, tulip, and violet.

If there are leftovers, or if the tart is made well ahead of serving time, store in the refrigerator.

LINDA'S CHOCOLATE TRUFFLE TORTE

*L*inda Schulak cooked at Cafe Pasqual's for many years. She is a graduate of La Varenne cooking school in Paris and her recipe for chocolate truffles is the best. When we began our dinner menu in 1987, I experimented with various chocolate torte recipes. But I was never truly satisfied until, one day, I realized that we already *had* the best chocolate concoction with Linda's French-inspired recipe. At Cafe Pasqual's we make a large quantity of the truffle recipe, spread it in a springform pan, and chill it. We serve slices of this rich, silken chocolate dessert with a dash of cocoa powder. *Voilà!* This just may be the only chocolate dessert recipe you will ever need.

Makes one 9-inch torte; serves 8 to 10

1 ½ **pounds semisweet chocolate**
   (see note)

2 **cups heavy cream**

2 **tablespoons unsalted butter**

High-quality unsweetened cocoa
   powder for dusting

Combine the chocolate, cream, and butter in the top pan of a double boiler over simmering water. Do not allow the chocolate to become too hot, or it will seize up and become hard and dry. When the chocolate mixture is completely melted, remove from the heat and whisk with a balloon whisk until all the ingredients are well incorporated.

Line the bottom of a 9-inch springform pan with waxed paper and pour the chocolate mixture into the pan. Let cool, cover, and chill for at least 6 hours or for up to 48 hours before serving.

To prepare the torte for serving, run the blade of a small, sharp pointed knife around the edge of the torte to loosen it from the sides of the pan. Unclasp and remove the ring from the springform pan. Run a long, flat icing spatula or similar implement between the torte and springform pan bottom to detach the torte. Invert a serving plate over the torte. Placing one hand beneath the springform pan bottom and one hand over the serving plate, invert so that the torte is resting on the serving plate. Remove the springform pan bottom and waxed paper from the top of the torte. Using a fine-mesh strainer or a fine-holed shaker, dust the top with cocoa powder.

To serve, slice into individual pieces and place on serving plates. Dust each serving again with cocoa powder. Refrigerate any leftovers.

Note: Ghirardelli-brand, semisweet chocolate bars, not bits, are highly recommended.

Ripe Figs with Marsala Cream Carroll

Carroll Johnson was the cafe's prep cook for five years. He was responsible for desserts during that time and created this truly elegant and sensual way to enjoy the fig. Sicilian Marsala is the dessert wine of Italy. It is a fortified wine with an earthy burnt-sugar flavor. Purchase dry Marsala rather than the more common sweet variety and make sure it is imported. You may find domestic Marsala, but it will not compare to a dark, deep, rich Italian vintage. Figs are best during high summer and into fall. Let them ripen and become somewhat soft before serving. You may want to double this recipe if the figs are very small.

Serves 4 to 8

1/2 cup heavy cream

**1 tablespoon confectioners' sugar
  (optional)**

1 to 2 tablespoons dry Marsala wine

**8 perfectly ripe white, green, or black
  figs, or a mixture**

Pour the cream into a mixing bowl. Using an electric mixer fitted with the whisk attachment, whip the cream until it becomes thick. Then add the sugar and continue to whip until stiff. Using a rubber spatula, fold in the Marsala wine, adding it to the cook's taste. Cover and refrigerate until serving.

To prepare each fig, cut off the tip of the stem flush with the fruit. To divide the fig into 8 radiating "star tips," cut straight down the center of the fruit from the stem *nearly* to the bottom. Do not cut all the way through; leave the fruit barely attached at the bottom. Next, make another bisecting cut to form quarters, then bisect the quartered fruit. You should now have an 8-pointed star attached at the center. All of the figs should be cut in this manner.

Spread out each star on an individual plate and fill with the cream. If you are serving 2 figs for each person, fill the first fig and then stack the second on top of the first and fill it. Position the tips of the second star so they are offset from the tips of the first, like a lotus flower.

Note: We always suggest to our diners that they may want to eat this with their fingers, dipping a point of the star into the cream for a more sensual experience.

Dessert at Cafe Pasqual's: Garnets in Blood, Chocolate Truffle Torte, and Bizcochitos.

GARNETS IN BLOOD

*P*omegranates are delicious, but it's hard to know how to use them. Here is an elegant treatment, a memorable dessert served to me by friends in Salamanca, Spain, one blustery fall evening. When we had finished eating our bountiful paella and cleared the dishes, dessert was served. Bowls, knives, spoons, and pomegranates were set on the table. A bottle of Rioja red wine and a bowl of sugar were placed in the middle of the table.

I watched with interest to see what to do next. With hardly a pause in the conversation, each person began to peel back the skin of a pomegranate and remove the seeds to a wide bowl. A teaspoon or so of sugar was added and then three or four good splashes of wine. We took up our spoons to stir our fruit "soup" and dissolve the sugar. Outside, the wind raged and the sky darkened as we, cozy inside, sipped our deep, red drink with its shiny floating "gems"—a glorious ending to a special repast.

This dessert was named by Judy Stone, who served dinners at Cafe Pasqual's some years ago. She had a flair for the dramatic and once complained that our dessert menu listing of Pomegranate in Rioja did not pique interest. So I said, "Well, you name it." Did she ever!

Serves 4

4 pomegranates

One-fifth Spanish Rioja wine

Granulated sugar

Empty the seeds of a pomegranate into each individual bowl. Divide the wine evenly among the bowls. Pass the sugar to give each guest an opportunity to sweeten to taste. Caution the diners to stir until the sugar is completely dissolved.

Note: Rioja, a wine from the north of Spain, is sold at most good wine shops. Ask your liquor dealer to help you choose a lively, fruity bottle. Pomegranates, called granadas in Spain, are available from mid-October through February. I choose the deep red ones for their beauty. These tough-skinned globes will keep for days before you have to use them.

SANGRÍA SORBET

*B*rad Brown, our general manager, made up this sorbet recipe one hot afternoon. Its wonderful dusky purple color is complemented by the green flecks of the essential fresh mint. You will find it perfect for summer entertaining. Feel free to experiment with the liquor content. We have used all manner of red wine, dreg ends, and even a splash of gin or tequila on occasion. Serve with *Bizcochitos* (page 151).

Serves 4 to 6

1 ½ **cups dry red wine**

1 **bottle (24 ounces) lemon lime soda**

1 **cantaloupe, peeled, seeded, and roughly cubed**

1/3 **cup fresh orange juice**

1/2 **cup lavender honey or other favorite honey**

8 **fresh mint leaves, stemmed and finely chopped**

Fresh mint sprigs and thin orange, lemon, and lime slices for garnish

Place all the ingredients, except the garnishes, in a food processor fitted with the metal blade. Process until smooth. Pour into an ice-cream maker and freeze according to the manufacturer's instructions.

To serve, garnish each bowl with the mint sprigs and fruit slices.

Note: Ice cream machines are quite inexpensive and are a happy addition to any kitchen's stock of equipment.

MEXICAN CHOCOLATE ICE CREAM

I have always loved the almond and cinnamon flavors of Mexican chocolate. The chocolate comes in tablet form and is, unfortunately, loaded with granulated sugar. For this recipe, Mexican chocolate is not recommended. At Cafe Pasqual's we have better results by simulating its flavors. The *chile pequín* flakes give the ice cream a kick into another dimension for chocolate lovers. This is a much-requested recipe and one I think you will find fun to serve.

Serves 6

3 cups half-and-half

1/2 cup firmly packed dark brown sugar

12 egg yolks, beaten

12 ounces semisweet chocolate

3 ounces unsweetened chocolate

2 tablespoons instant coffee powder

3 tablespoons ground cinnamon

3/4 cup confectioners' sugar

1 cup blanched almonds, lightly toasted and coarsely crushed

1 teaspoon *pequín* chile flakes

1 cup Kahlúa liqueur

In a saucepan over medium heat, combine 2 cups of the half-and-half and the brown sugar. Heat, stirring frequently, until the sugar dissolves completely.

Remove the pan from the heat. Whisk 1/3 cup of the sugar mixture into the egg yolks to warm them slightly. Return the sugar mixture to the heat and stir in the slightly heated egg yolks. Continue to cook, stirring constantly with a wooden spoon, until the mixture is thickened enough to coat the back of the spoon, 15 to 20 minutes. Remove from the heat and strain through a fine-mesh strainer into a bowl. Set aside.

Combine seven ounces of the semisweet chocolate, all of the unsweetened chocolate, and the coffee together in the top pan of a double boiler over simmering water and heat until melted. Scrape the chocolate mixture into the bowl of a food processor fitted with the plastic blade. Add the remaining 1 cup half-and-half, the cinnamon, and confectioners' sugar. Process until smooth, then transfer to a bowl. Gradually add the chocolate mixture to the custard, stirring to mix well. Let cool to room temperature, about 30 minutes.

Pour the cooled chocolate mixture into an ice-cream maker and freeze according to the manufacturer's instructions until the ice cream is thick and creamy, about 30 minutes. Coarsely chop the remaining 5 ounces semisweet chocolate and stir it into the ice cream along with the almonds and chile flakes.

To serve, divide the ice cream among individual bowls and pour the Kahlúa evenly over the servings.

TOASTED PIÑON ICE CREAM

*T*his recipe is our number one best-selling dessert and was requested so often that it is now a daily item. Piñon nuts (pine nuts) are costly, so I suggest you purchase them in bulk from a natural-food market or order them through the mail. This recipe does not require an ice cream machine.

Serves 6 to 8

1/2 cup piñon nuts

3 cups heavy cream

12 egg yolks

2 teaspoons ground cinnamon

2 teaspoons vanilla extract

1 cup granulated sugar

1¼ cups plus 2 tablespoons water

Ice cream topping of your choice such
    as caramel, chocolate, or
    butterscotch (optional)

Preheat an oven to 250° F.

Spread the nuts on a baking sheet and place in the oven. Toast, stirring frequently, until pale brown, 8 to 10 minutes. Watch to see they do not burn. Remove from the oven when they are toasted but not too dark, as they will continue to cook as they cool. Set aside.

Put the cream in a large bowl and whip until stiff. Cover and refrigerate.

Put the egg yolks, cinnamon, and vanilla extract in a bowl. Using an electric mixer fitted with the whip attachment, whip on medium speed until light yellow and thickened, about 5 minutes. Set aside.

In a small, heavy-bottomed saucepan, combine the sugar and the 1¼ cups water. Bring it to a boil over high heat, stirring constantly, then stop stirring so that the sugar doesn't crystallize. Let the syrup cook without stirring until it caramelizes and becomes deep amber. This may take as long as 20 to 25 minutes.

Remove from the heat and carefully add the 2 tablespoons water, stirring constantly with a balloon whisk until smooth. The syrup may splatter when the water is added, so be sure to wear a long-sleeved garment for this stage and have anyone else who is present stand back.

With the mixer set on high speed, slowly drizzle the caramelized syrup into the yolk mixture. Continue to beat until the mixture cools to room temperature and is as thick as the whipped cream.

Gently fold the syrup-yolk mixture into the whipped cream. Stir in the nuts. Remove to a freezer container, cover tightly, and immediately put into the freezer. Allow it to freeze hard before serving, 6 to 8 hours.

Serve the ice cream with or without a favorite topping.

Manager Brad Brown, Cafe Pasqual's.

LAVENDER-HONEY ICE CREAM

*T*his rich, yet delicate ice cream came about after my first trip to Provence. That trip to France was at the height of summer, when all the lavender is in its majestic purple bloom. Lavender has always been a favorite flower of mine, so I returned home inspired, and, with the help of Linda Schulak, our pastry chef, set about developing a recipe to celebrate the herb. The most successful of those early efforts was lavender flowers steeped in cream; the result was all right, but not quite evocative enough. Then, on a trip to my hometown of Berkeley, California, I stopped in at the shop of renowned wine merchant Kermit Lynch, and there I spied a pyramid of jars of French lavender honey. A gift from the bees of Provence—and the missing essence! Treat yourself and do as we do at Cafe Pasqual's: Send for some jars (you need only one, but stock up) and make this ice cream. Then sit back in a comfortable armchair with a dish of the creamy, fragrant stuff and allow your senses to transport you to the lavender fields of southern France. *Bizcochitos* (page 151) are delicious served with the ice cream.

Serves 8

6 cups heavy cream

**2 tablespoons plus 2 teaspoons
pesticide-free lavender flowers,
stemmed (see note)**

1 ½ cups lavender honey

15 egg yolks

Pour the cream into a saucepan over medium heat and heat until very hot but not boiling. Turn off the heat and stir in the 2 tablespoons lavender flowers. Let steep for 20 minutes. Add the honey and stir well.

In a large bowl, beat the egg yolks with a wire whisk until well incorporated. Pour 1/4 cup of the hot cream mixture into the egg yolks, whisking constantly. Repeat with another 1/4 cup of the cream. Then pour the egg mixture into the cream mixture, whisking well.

Put the yolk-cream mixture in the top pan of a double boiler over gently simmering water. Heat, stirring constantly with a wooden spoon, until thick enough to coat the back of the spoon. Be careful not to curdle the mixture by overheating. Pour the mixture through a fine-mesh strainer into a bowl and discard the lavender flowers. Let cool.

Pour into an ice-cream maker and freeze according to the manufacturer's instructions.

To serve, divide the ice cream among individual bowls and sprinkle the remaining 2 teaspoons lavender flowers evenly over the servings.

Note: Lavender flowers may be purchased at herb stores or natural-food markets.

BIZCOCHITOS

*T*his simple rolled cookie has marked history in New Mexico on more than one occasion. At one time, it was said these aniseed cookies were commonly cut in the shape of a fleur-de-lys, to honor the French origins of Archbishop Lamy who oversaw the building of Santa Fe's cathedral. A few years ago the New Mexico state legislature voted to make the *bizcochito* the state cookie! Lard has been the traditional shortening for this recipe. Other shortenings may be substituted with nontraditional results. We serve *bizcochitos* daily as an accompaniment to our ice creams.

Makes about 24 cookies

1 cup (1/2 pound) lard, margarine, unsalted butter (at room temperature), or solid vegetable shortening

1/2 cup plus 2 tablespoons granulated sugar

1 teaspoon aniseeds

2 egg yolks

1/4 cup fresh orange juice

1 1/2 teaspoons baking powder

3 cups all-purpose flour

3 to 4 tablespoons solid vegetable shortening or nonstick spray coating for baking sheet

1 tablespoon ground cinnamon

Preheat an oven to 350° F.

Combine the lard or other fat and the 1/2 cup sugar in a bowl. Using a wooden spoon or an electric mixer fitted with the paddle attachment set on high speed, cream together until well incorporated. Beat in

the aniseeds and then the egg yolks until thoroughly blended.

Reduce the mixer speed to low and, with the mixer running, add the orange juice, baking powder, and, finally, the flour, mixing just long enough to incorporate the flour.

Lightly grease a baking sheet. Divide the dough into 2 balls. On a floured board, roll out each ball 1/4 inch thick. Using a 2 1/2- to 3-inch cookie cutter, cut out the cookies. Place the cutouts on the prepared baking sheet, spacing them about 1/2 inch apart. Sprinkle the cookies with cinnamon and the 2 tablespoons sugar.

Place in the oven and bake until very lightly browned, 8 to 10 minutes. Remove from the oven and let cool on racks. The cookies may be stored in an airtight container at room temperature for 3 to 4 days.

FULL MOON COOKIES

My mother made these cookies when I was a kid and she called them Mexican wedding cookies. My father-in-law called them Russian tea cookies. Now I make them extra large to celebrate the full moon, hence their name at Cafe Pasqual's. I love to serve these alongside fresh raspberries or strawberries: the wet scarlet of the berries is a gorgeous contrast to the powdery white of the cookies. The next time you want to celebrate the full moon or a circle of friends, try this delicious sweet.

Makes 12 large cookies

1 cup (1/2 pound) unsalted butter, at room temperature

3 cups confectioners' sugar

2 teaspoons vanilla extract

3/4 cup finely chopped pecans

3/4 teaspoon salt

2¼ cups all-purpose flour

3 tablespoons solid vegetable shortening or nonstick spray coating for baking sheet

Preheat an oven to 375° F.

Combine the butter and 2½ cups of the confectioners' sugar in a bowl. Using a whisk, a wooden spoon, or an electric mixer fitted with the paddle attachment set on high speed, cream together until well incorporated. Add the vanilla extract, pecans, salt, and flour and beat just until blended.

Lightly grease a baking sheet. Divide the dough into 12 equal pieces. Between lightly floured palms, roll each piece into a ball. Place the balls on the prepared baking sheet. Place in the oven and bake until the cookies are light brown on the bottom, 12 to 15 minutes.

Remove from the oven and let cool slightly on a rack. While the cookies are still warm but not hot, roll them in some of the remaining 1/2 cup confectioners' sugar to coat completely. Set aside to cool on a rack. When cool, roll again in the sugar until well coated and evenly powdered. The cookies may be stored in an airtight tin at room temperature for up to 7 days.

Apple-cheeked young girl samples a Yellow Delicious apple at the annual Velarde Valley Apple Festival, Velarde, New Mexico.

MAIL-ORDER SOURCES

Cafe Pasqual's, 121 Don Gaspar, Santa Fe, NM 87501; (800) 722-7672, Fax (505) 988-4645.
Products from Pasqual's Pantry and Cafe: Curiosities and Delectables. Call or send for our catalog.

A-1 Produce, West Airport Road, Santa Fe, NM 87505; (505) 471-5400, Fax (505) 471-5803.
Fresh chiles in season.

Balducci's, 424 Avenue of the Americas, New York, NY 10011; (800) 225-3822.
Vinegars, cheeses. Catalog available.

Bangkok Grocery, 1021 West Lawrence, Chicago, IL 60640; (312) 784-0001, Fax (312) 784-2904.
Thai chiles, lemongrass, Thai fish sauce, kaffir lime leaves.

Blue Sky, 1570 Center Court, Unit A, Santa Fe, NM 87505; (800) 742-2756.
Piñon nuts, walnuts, pecan halves.

Casados Farms, P.O. Box 852, San Juan Pueblo, NM 87566; (505) 852-2433.
Husks, chile pods and powders, spices, blue cornmeal. Catalog available.

The Chile Shop, 109 East Water Street, Santa Fe, NM 87501; (505) 983-6080, Fax (505) 984-0737.
Dried chiles of all types, Chimayó chile powder, *ristras*, blue corn products. Catalog available.

Coyote Cafe General Store, 132 West Water Street, Santa Fe, NM 87501; (800) 866-HOWL, Fax (505) 989-9026.
Dried chiles, beans, nuts, herbs, spices. Catalog available.

Dean & Deluca, 560 Broadway, New York, NY 10012; (800) 221-7714, Fax (212) 334-6183.
Kaffir lime leaves, lemongrass, Thai fish sauce, Thai chiles.

Desert Grove, Drawer BB, Las Cruces, NM 88004; (800) 654-6887, Fax (505) 526-7824.
Pecan halves. Catalog available.

Gallina Canyon Ranch, Elizabeth Berry, 144 Camino Escondito, Santa Fe, NM 87501; (505) 982-4149.
Beans, chile seeds, fresh squash blossoms.

Harrods, 87–135 Brompton Road, London, SW1XL, England; (44) 71-730-1234
Thai chiles and other Thai ingredients.

Josie's Best, P.O. Box 5525, Santa Fe, NM 87502; (505) 473-3437.
Frozen green chiles, frozen red chiles, *posole*, tortillas, chile powder and pods. Frozen and fresh products shipped by UPS Overnight and 2nd Day services. Catalog available.

Kam Man Food Products, 200 Canal Street, New York, NY 10013; (212) 571-0330, Fax (212) 766-9085.
Lemongrass, Thai chiles, Thai fish sauce.

Kermit Lynch Wine Merchant, 1605 San Pablo Avenue, Berkeley, CA 94702-1317; (510) 524-1524, Fax (510) 528-7026.
Lavender honey, olive oil, olives. Exquisite wine. Newsletter available.

La Palma, 2884 24th Street, San Francisco, CA 94110; (415) 647-1500, Fax (415) 647-1710.
Dried chiles, Mexican spices. Catalog available.

Léona's de Chimayó, P.O. Box 579, Chimayó, NM 87522; (800)-4-LEONAS.
Whole-wheat tortillas, vegetarian tamales, flavored tortillas. Fresh products shipped by UPS Overnight and 2nd Day services. Catalog available.

Los Chileros, P.O. Box 6215, Santa Fe, NM 87502; (505) 471-6967, Fax (505) 473-7306.
Chiles, piñon nuts, *chicos*, *posole*. Catalog available.

Mi Rancho Tortilla Factory, 464 7th Street, Oakland, CA 94607; (510) 451-2393.
Ibarra Mexican chocolate, *masa*, chiles, spices. Catalog available.

Monterrey Food Products, 3939 Brooklyn Avenue, Los Angeles, CA 90063; (213) 263-2143, Fax (213) 263-2545.
Ibarra Mexican chocolate, *achiote* paste, dried chiles, *chipotles*, black beans, cooking equipment. Catalog available.

The Mozzarella Company, 2944 Elm Street, Dallas, TX 75226; (800) 798-2954, Fax (214) 741-4076.
Fresh butter, fresh mozzarella, *mascarpone*, *queso blanco*, goat cheese. Fresh products shipped by UPS Overnight and 2nd Day services. Catalog available.

Nueske Hillcrest Farm Meats, RR 2, Wittenberg, WI 54499; (800) 38-BACON, Fax (715) 253-2021.
Bacon, sausages, duck, ham, pork loin. Fresh products shipped by UPS Overnight and 2nd Day services. Catalog available.

Old Southwest Trading Company, P.O. Box 7545, Albuquerque, NM 97194; (505) 836-0618.
Southwest ingredients, fresh chiles in season, dried and exotic New Mexico chiles.

Perfecto Products, 3000 4th NW, Albuquerque, NM 87107; (505) 345-2144.
Piñon nuts, dried red chiles.

Port of Siam, 5400 Highway 17 S, Myrtle Beach, SC 29575; (803) 238-2658.
Lemongrass, Thai chiles, kaffir lime leaves, Thai fish sauce.

Reynoso Brothers Food, 14273 East Don Julian, City of Industry, CA 91746; (818) 330-1999, Fax (818) 330-4222.
Dried chiles, Mexican cheese, Mexican chocolate, banana leaves.

Ta Lin Supermarket, 230 Louisiana Boulevard SE, Albuquerque, NM 87108; (505) 268-0206.
Thai chiles, kaffir lime leaves, lemongrass, banana leaves, Thai fish sauce. Will ship prepaid.

T & R Enterprises, P.O. Box 3743, Santa Fe, NM 87501-0743; (505) 661-8112, Fax (505) 988-4537.
All dried chiles.

Zingerman's Delicatessen, 422 Detroit Street, Ann Arbor, MI 48104; (313) 663-DELI.
Balsamic vinegars, olive oils, cheeses. Catalog available.

TABLE OF EQUIVALENTS

The exact equivalents in the following tables have been rounded for convenience.

US/UK

oz=ounce
lb=pound
in=inch
ft=foot
tbl=tablespoon
fl oz=fluid ounce
qt=quart

Metric

g=gram
kg=kilogram
mm=millimeter
cm=centimeter
ml=milliliter
l=liter

Weights

US/UK	Metric
1 oz	30 g
2 oz	60 g
3 oz	90 g
4 oz (1/4 lb)	125 g
5 oz (1/3 lb)	155 g
6 oz	185 g
7 oz	220 g
8 oz (1/2 lb)	250 g
10 oz	315 g
12 oz (3/4 lb)	375 g
14 oz	440 g
16 oz (1 lb)	500 g
1 1/2 lb	750 g
2 lb	1 kg
3 lb	1.5 kg

Oven Temperatures

Fahrenheit	Celsius	Gas
250	120	1/2
275	140	1
300	150	2
325	160	3
350	180	4
375	190	5
400	200	6
425	220	7
450	230	8
475	240	9
500	260	10

Liquids

US	Metric	UK
2 tbl	30 ml	1 fl oz
1/4 cup	60 ml	2 fl oz
1/3 cup	80 ml	3 fl oz
1/2 cup	125 ml	4 fl oz
2/3 cup	160 ml	5 fl oz
3/4 cup	180 ml	6 fl oz
1 cup	250 ml	8 fl oz
1 1/2 cups	375 ml	12 fl oz
2 cups	500 ml	16 fl oz
4 cups/1 qt	1 l	32 fl oz

Equivalents for Commonly Used Ingredients

All-Purpose (Plain) Flour/ Dried Bread Crumbs/Chopped Nuts

1/4 cup	1 oz	30 g
1/3 cup	1 1/2 oz	45 g
1/2 cup	2 oz	60 g
3/4 cup	3 oz	90 g
1 cup	4 oz	125 g
1 1/2 cups	6 oz	185 g
2 cups	8 oz	250 g

Whole-Wheat (Wholemeal) Flour

3 tbl	1 oz	30 g
1/2 cup	2 oz	60 g
2/3 cup	3 oz	90 g
1 cup	4 oz	125 g
1 1/4 cups	5 oz	155 g
1 2/3 cups	7 oz	210 g
1 3/4 cups	8 oz	250 g

Brown Sugar

1/4 cup	1 1/2 oz	45 g
1/2 cup	3 oz	90 g
3/4 cup	4 oz	125 g
1 cup	5 1/2 oz	170 g
1 1/2 cups	8 oz	250 g
2 cups	10 oz	315 g

White Sugar

1/4 cup	2 oz	60 g
1/3 cup	3 oz	90 g
1/2 cup	4 oz	125 g
3/4 cup	6 oz	185 g
1 cup	8 oz	250 g
1 1/2 cups	12 oz	375 g
2 cups	1 lb	500 g

Long-Grain Rice/Cornmeal

1/3 cup	2 oz	60 g
1/2 cup	2 1/2 oz	75 g
3/4 cup	4 oz	125 g
1 cup	5 oz	155 g
1 1/2 cups	8 oz	250 g

Dried Beans

1/4 cup	1 1/2 oz	45 g
1/3 cup	2 oz	60 g
1/2 cup	3 oz	90 g
3/4 cup	5 oz	155 g
1 cup	6 oz	185 g
1 1/4 cups	8 oz	250 g
1 1/2 cups	12 oz	375 g

INDEX